ESSENTIAL VEGETABLE FERMENTATION

ESSENTIAL
VEGETABLE
FERMENTATION

70 Inventive Recipes to Make Your Own Pickles, Kraut, Kimchi, and More

KELLY McVICKER

Photography by Andrew Purcell

ROCKRIDGE
PRESS

Interior and Cover Designer: John Clifford
Art Producer: Hannah Dickerson
Editor: Sam Eichner
Production Editor: Ruth Sakata Corley

Photography © 2019 Andrew Purcell, Food styling by Carrie Purcell; Illustrations Shutterstock, pp. 4–5 and @ Tom Bingham, pp. 25–26, 29–30
Author photo courtesy of Alejandro Morales

ISBN: Print 978-1-64611-526-6 | eBook 978-1-64611-527-3

RO

For Alejandro

Contents

Introduction

I have always been an adventurous and unfussy eater, but sauerkraut was one of the few things I truly *hated* as a kid. Even though I grew up in a part of Kansas with a significant German immigrant population, I had never tried a freshly fermented sauerkraut until I moved to California. I can't even say that I liked it then. The smell, and the sour complexity, was totally unfamiliar to my palate.

When I founded my pickling business, McVicker Pickles, in 2012, I still didn't like sauerkraut, and I knew very little about fermentation. My pickling knowledge was entirely vinegar-based, coming largely from my grandmas, Margarett and Harriet, who used vinegar pickling for more practical than nutritional purposes (this was quite clear to me simply from the amount of sugar used in some of their recipes).

As my taste buds evolved and the microbes got their hold on me, I slowly (and then, very quickly) came around to all things fermented. Now, not a day goes by that I don't consume fermented vegetables of some variety, whether it's my morning shot of beet kvass or a few bites of kimchi. The complex flavors of fermented foods have a way of making us want to come back for more. And that is not by accident.

Fermentation is an ancient process that predates written records in many parts of the world. By observing how fermentation happened naturally and then developing ways to control the process, humans have co-evolved with the very microbes that nurture us in a mutually beneficial collaboration.

Ever since the development of germ theory in the middle of the 19th century and the subsequent discovery of antibiotics, our relationship with bacteria has been more adversarial than collaborative. As we learn more about how bacteria impacts our health, our culture is coming to a more balanced understanding that does not cast all bacteria as something to be eradicated or sterilized. Evidence of that shift is apparent at most modern grocery stores, where the shelves are packed with probiotic-rich kimchi, yogurt, sauerkraut, and kombucha.

While there are many different types of fermented foods, each with their own unique flavors, appeals, and benefits, this book focuses exclusively on fermenting vegetables. On the whole, no other fermentation technique provides so much benefit in exchange for relatively little effort. Fermenting vegetables at home requires far less investment than other fermentation projects like homebrewing and cheesemaking. There are no special bacteria cultures to buy, no incubation chambers to build, and no stringent sterilization procedures to follow.

Almost magically, vegetables contain all the life they need to begin fermenting on their own, given the right conditions. All you need is salt, a jar, and an understanding of the basic elements that will make your fermentation a success.

IF YOU'RE A BEGINNER

I know that fermentation can seem intimidating at first. If that's the case for you, you're not alone! Our current food system has a way of making people feel that fermentation is a scary, complicated process best left to the pros. I couldn't disagree more. As an experienced commercial pickle producer, I actually believe fermentation is better suited to the home kitchen than to an industrial one. In **chapters 1, 2, and 3**, I'll ground you with a basic understanding of how fermentation works and equip you with practical techniques and recipes to explore the process on your own.

IF YOU'RE READY FOR THE RECIPES

For those with experience fermenting vegetables, **you can skip the first few chapters and move right on to chapters 4 through 9**. Maybe you're an experienced pickle maker, but have never delved into leafy greens (see chapter 6, page 81). Perhaps you're a spice maestro, but want to learn how to make some pastes to liven up your rice bowls (see chapter 8, page 109). Wherever you're starting from, it's my hope that you find something new to incorporate into your fermentation repertoire.

CHAPTER ONE

THE MAGIC OF FERMENTATION

In this chapter we'll dive into the history of fermentation and the science that makes it all happen. You'll learn about the benefits that fermentation can impart on ecosystems big and small: how it works in the jar, how it works in your body, and how it can even work to create a healthier planet by reducing food waste and the energy required to prepare and preserve food.

OF COURSE, IT ALL STARTED WITH WINE . . .

The Romans took one look at the bubbling that occurs when yeast converts the juice from grapes or other fruit into wine, and, perhaps drunkenly, assigned the phenomenon its current name, using the Latin verb *fervere*—or "to boil."

Yet fermentation far predates the linguistically endowed Romans. The oldest evidence we have goes back 9,000 years: Residue found on pottery fragments from this time suggests that Neolithic people living in what's now western China kicked back with an alcoholic beverage fermented from rice, fruit, and honey.

Some evidence points to central Asia as the origin site of yogurt, one of our most famous fermented foods, around 6,000 BCE. More recent evidence suggests that it may have originated in northern Africa even earlier than that, when camel herders draped sheepskin bags over their camels and filled them with milk. In that scenario, the heat, combined with the enzymes on the animal skins, caused the milk to curdle, thus creating yogurt.

Regardless of where and when it actually began, people recognized right away the benefit of turning milk into yogurt, just as they recognized the benefit of turning grape juice into wine: It lasted longer. Once they adjusted to the sour taste, it became more desirable than its milky predecessor.

Early spontaneous ferments gave rise to a range of foods—bread, cheese, vinegar, cured meats, pickles, and more. But it would take several thousand more years for people to understand what was causing these transformations to occur. In the mid-1800s, the French chemist Louis Pasteur finally made the connection between yeast and the process of fermentation. Through his laboratory work, he observed that fermentation occurred in anaerobic (or oxygenless) environments, leading him to define it, rather poetically, as "respiration without air."

A little after the turn of the 20th century, a Russian microbiologist named Élie Metchnikoff was studying Bulgarians. He wanted to find out why they had a higher life expectancy than other cultures—87 years, an unusually high number for that time. His research led him to believe that it was the large amounts of yogurt and kefir people tended to consume, especially in rural areas. He focused on a particular strain of bacteria, which he isolated and named *Lactobacillus bulgaricus*.

Subsequent researchers showed that this type of bacteria couldn't quite cut it in the acids of our digestive system. But other lactic acid bacteria, they found, could not only survive—they could thrive.

This understanding of bacteria paved the way for renewed interest in probiotic foods. Today, the combination of nostalgia for our ancestral foods and interest in the health benefits they provide are driving more and more people to reach for jars of kimchi, kombucha, and fermented pickles of all kinds.

Fermentation may be trendy, but it has no expiration date. It continues to expand our palate—and, naturally, we find ourselves wanting more.

Fermentation Around the World

All over the world, people have discovered different ways of using fermentation to preserve food, transform its flavors, and incorporate it into their daily lives.

In places where the growing season is short, with long, harsh winters, the primary benefit of fermentation was, well, survival. People preserved food so there would be something to eat during the months when nothing would grow. By contrast, folks in more moderate and tropical climates, where fruits and vegetables were abundant year-round, didn't depend on fermentation as a preserver as much as a means of adding flavor or turning one food product (e.g., milk) into another (e.g., cheese).

Today, there is no human culture on the planet that does not employ these feisty microbes to preserve and transform food in some way. Here are some of the most well-known examples.

Greenland/Inuit Community
Kiviak (sea birds stuffed into the carcass of a seal, then buried in the ground to ferment)

United States
Sourdough (bread fermented using *Lactobacillus* culture in combination with yeasts)

Mexico
Atole Agrio (a thick beverage made from fermented black maize dough)

El Salvador
Curtido (fermented vegetable slaw of cabbage, carrots, peppers, onions, garlic, and spices)

Peru/Andean States
Chicha (fermented beverage, typically made from corn or maize)

Russia
Kvass (a fermented beverage made from bread yeast or wild fermented beets)

Germany and Eastern Europe
Sauerkraut (shredded cabbage, frequently mixed with other vegetables and spices)

Turkey
Ayran (a cold fermented drink consisting of yogurt, water, and salt)

Iran
Torshi (mixed vegetable medley served on the side with meals, also frequently vinegar-cured)

Korea (North and South)
Kimchi (mixture of any fermented vegetables, most often including cabbage, chili powder, ginger, and garlic)

Japan
Natto (fermented soybeans used as topping)

Syria/Lebanon/Egypt
Shanklish (cheese made from cow or sheep's milk, rolled into balls, and covered with spices; used with eggs or as a pita topping)

Sudan
Furundu (black sesame seeds fermented with salt and water, then pressed into cakes)

Ethiopia and Eritrea
Injera (sour bread made from fermented teff grain)

India and Sri Lanka
Idli (fermented and steamed rice and black bean cakes)

Thailand
Chin Som Mok (pork fermented with sticky rice, then wrapped in banana leaf and grilled)

Philippines
Bagoong (sauce made from fermented fish or shrimp)

Indonesia
Tempeh (live mold added to soybean, then fermented into a nutritious cake)

WHAT'S ACTUALLY HAPPENING DURING FERMENTATION?

Beginning with the broadest scientific definition, fermentation refers to the process by which a microorganism metabolizes sugar in the absence of oxygen. The sugar feeds the microbes, which then create specific by-products, depending on the type of fermentation used and the desired result. In the culinary context, fermentation is the metabolic transformation that takes place when microbes—generally bacteria and yeasts—act upon the carbohydrate (sugar) content of foods.

Let's break it down into a few different types relevant to fermenting food and beverages.

Acetic fermentation works by transforming alcohol into acetic acid through the action of *Acetobacter*, a specific bacteria strain. This is how vinegar is made from corn, apples, and grapes.

Amylolytic fermentation relies on acids and the specific amylase enzyme to turn starches into simple sugars. This process is commonly used in brewing alcohol from grain. Since most grains have starches but not simple sugars, the amylolytic process is necessary to feed the fermentation by first turning starches into sugars.

Once that's done, **alcoholic fermentation** can begin. When the initial ingredient has a high sugar content (such as grapes used for wine), alcoholic fermentation begins quickly because the sugars are abundant and readily available.

When we are fermenting vegetables, we are using a specific process called **lacto-fermentation**. The term *lacto* has nothing to do with dairy; it refers instead to lactic acid bacteria, which acidifies the food and transforms its flavor.

Most lacto-fermentation is easy to achieve via spontaneous, or wild, fermentation. This simply means that rather than having to use a starter (such as a kombucha SCOBY, vinegar mother, or a yogurt culture), we rely on the inherent bacteria and yeasts living inside of the vegetables to fuel fermentation. If we were gardening, wild fermentation would be like pulling weeds in a field of wildflowers, whereas starter-culture fermentation is more like pruning a neat row of hybrid roses.

The fermentation process alters food in a number of ways:

- The texture changes as enzymes produced by the microbes break down the cell structures of the vegetable being fermented, softening it in the process. This means the difference between a crunchy cabbage and a softer, more pliable sauerkraut.

- The taste is transformed as these same enzymes break down large chains of molecules into amino acids and simple sugars. Once that happens, a whole new world of flavor opens up because our bodies can more easily recognize the sweet, funky, and umami flavors that were previously undetectable in the larger molecules.

- From a nutritional perspective, fermentation is magical. It takes already healthy veggies and transforms them into superfoods (see page 9).

Ultimately, fermentation results in complex, deeply satisfying flavors that really can't be achieved any other way. And that's by nature's design. Just as flowers evolve their brilliant colors to entice bees to visit, microbes active in the fermentation process break down starches and proteins into components that are tastier to humans than their nonfermented origins. Symbiosis at its finest!

The Wonderful Simplicity of Lacto-Fermentation

The recipes in this book deal exclusively with lacto-fermentation. While many types of fermentation offer varied health benefits, unpasteurized lacto-fermented foods are the only ones that can truly be called probiotic, meaning that they contain health-enhancing bacteria that stay present in the food throughout the life of the ferment. For example, though sourdough contains lactic acid bacteria, the high temperature of the cooking process kills them off.

So, how specifically does lacto-fermentation work with vegetables?

After we add salt to vegetables, submerge them in brine (creating an anaerobic environment), and allow them to sit at room temperature, two things start to happen. First, the salt inhibits further growth of bacteria that would cause the vegetables to decompose, buying a little window of time in which *Lactobacillus* and other acid-loving bacteria can assert their dominance. Microbes collaborate, but they also compete, and they're constantly duking it out for primacy in any given ecosystem.

As these lactic acid bacteria (commonly referred to as *LAB*) flourish and multiply, they secrete even *more* lactic acid, which further acidifies the environment in a fermentation vessel. That acidification makes the environment inhospitable to pathogens (like mold) that would cause it to putrefy—they simply can't compete with their acid-loving counterparts. All of this makes the fermented result more resistant to spoilage and microbial toxins like *E. coli*, and less likely to harbor pathogenic organisms in general.

But hold on a sec. Let's back up—how did those LAB get there in the first place? The answer is that they were there all along, hanging out in the soil along with billions of other bacteria from various strains. Just like us, vegetables are living organisms, teeming with billions of other living organisms in, on, and around them.

WHY ARE FERMENTED FOODS
SO GOOD FOR YOU?

It may not be very appealing to think of bacteria chewing on your food before it makes its way to you, but it's this action that achieves one of fermentation's key benefits: transforming complex foods into the simple nutrients our bodies need. In other words, fermentation predigests your food for you—sounds gross, but it benefits your body.

Fermentation also generates new nutrients. Vitamins B and C, in particular, are increased during fermentation, which is why already healthy cabbage turns into a superfood when it's made into sauerkraut or kimchi. B vitamins impact your body's energy levels, metabolism, and brain function, while vitamin C helps fend off infection and promotes healthy tissue growth. There's a growing body of research demonstrating how eating fermented foods can benefit your mental health, too.

Yet as magical as fermentation is, it's not a cure-all. It's difficult to predict what impact even 10 billion microbes present in a cup of yogurt will have on your digestive health, if any. So rather than limiting yourself to one food or supplement, the best approach is to eat a broad range of fermented foods—and to be realistic about the results.

The Pros of Probiotics

Probiotic foods contain good bacteria, which can benefit your health in a variety of ways.

Improved digestion Eating probiotic-rich food populates your gut flora with bacteria that do a better job of breaking down proteins.

Enhanced immunity Early lab trials show that probiotics may help fight off parasitic infections in the intestines while strengthening the gut's mucus barrier and supporting overall immune defenses.

Easier nutrient absorption Fermentation breaks down food, making it easier for your body to access nutrients while also generating new nutrients in the process.

Better mood An ever-growing body of research exploring the intimate connection between the gut and the brain (known as the *gut-brain axis*) shows that the type of bacteria in our gut can have a huge impact on our mood and behavior. Cultures with a probiotic-rich diet tend to have lower levels of anxiety, depression, ADHD, and other chronic mental health issues.

THE FUTURE OF FERMENTATION

Our modern food system is impressive in its complexity and global scale. It's also incredibly wasteful: According to the National Resources Defense Council, up to 40 percent of food produced in the United States ends up in the landfill, with 43 percent of that waste occurring at the household level. Because this food breaks down anaerobically, it ends up releasing methane into the atmosphere—a much more potent greenhouse gas than carbon dioxide.

With food shortages exacerbated by climate crises and geopolitical uncertainty, we must find ways to not just produce *more* food, but to produce *more nutritious* food. When it comes to wild fermentation, soil health really matters. We're relying on bacteria and yeast that come from the soil, so it makes sense that healthy, nutrient-rich soil will make for healthier veggies and, ultimately, healthier ferments. The microbiome in the soil beneath our feet and the microbiomes in our bodies operate in a similar way— accessing nutrients and breaking them down through the use of bacteria and fungi. Hyperlocal ferments retain the microbial fingerprint of their homeplace, just like honey includes pollen collected from the plants and trees around the beehive where it came from.

Currently, nutrition scientists are exploring fermented foods as part of the solution for food shortages and malnutrition, because they allow for more nutrients to be packed into less space. On an individual basis, fermentation allows us to take raw food and transform it into something with more nutrition and a longer lifespan without requiring energy-intensive cooking or freezing.

These days, it's natural to feel powerless in the face of our warming planet. But fermenting your own food at home is a small yet not insignificant way to make the world a better place—and eat well in the process.

CHAPTER TWO

THE FERMENTATION-FRIENDLY KITCHEN

In this chapter, you'll learn everything you need to know to create a successful vegetable fermentation setup at home. You'll learn how light, temperature, and time influence the process in subtle but important ways. I'll demystify the equipment involved, detailing what you definitely need (and what you can live without). By the end, you'll be ready to tackle your first ferment. That's when the real education will begin.

PREPPING YOUR KITCHEN FOR FERMENTATION

Fermenting vegetables at home requires far less investment than other fermentation projects, like homebrewing and cheesemaking.

To begin with, it's important to clean your surfaces and utensils. You can do this by mixing a simple 1:1 white vinegar and water solution. Avoid using antibacterial soap or bleach-based cleansers, as these can inhibit fermentation.

Other than equipment, the most significant investment you'll make in fermenting is time. The good news is that most of the time spent isn't actively doing anything. After packing your jars and placing them in a good spot—ideally in a corner or high shelf, given they can produce pungent aromas—you can go on with your everyday life while your jars happily bubble and burp on your countertop.

The Equipment

Fermenting vegetables via lacto-fermentation is a great entry point for folks who are entranced by the magic of the microbes, but who would prefer not to mess around with too many gadgets and complicated setups—i.e., folks like me.

Most of these things you likely already have in your kitchen. Throughout the recipes, I'll also give hacks for using common kitchen items to achieve the same thing that the more expensive gadgets do.

Beyond that, there are a few tools that can make your fermentation projects easier and reduce the risk of spoilage. They can be purchased at kitchen stores or online.

MUST HAVE

- Glass jars with tight-fitting lids

- Sharp chef's knife

- Large (and extra-large) bowls

- Fermentation weights (especially for smaller ferments and pastes)

- Funnel (for sauces)

- Food processor or immersion blender

- Mesh strainer

- Food-grade gloves (for hot sauces)

- Fermentation journal or notebook

WEIGHTS AND AIR LOCKS

As your jar sits out to ferment at room temperature, any vegetables that pop up above the brine greatly increase the likelihood of spoilage. **Fermentation weights** made just for this purpose are available in home goods stores and online, but you can also use cabbage leaves, large pieces of other vegetables, or a heavy duty zip-top bag, filled with water and sealed, to weigh your vegetables down. **Air locks**—a one-way valve that allows gases to escape but doesn't let air in, similar to the ones used for homebrewing—are also helpful in minimizing air exposure, making your ferments more foolproof.

NICE TO HAVE

- Air lock

- Box grater or microplane

- Electric spice grinder or coffee grinder

- Crock (useful for fermenting larger volumes of vegetables for longer periods of time)

- Heavy-duty zip-top bags

- pH strips (for measuring acidity)

The Environment

The fermentation process draws from the environment around it. Beyond using high-quality produce and spices (organic whenever possible) and maintaining a clean and well-organized kitchen, there are three factors that will determine the results of your ferment.

TEMPERATURE

The microbes we want to invite to the fermentation jar do their best work in ambient temperatures between 65°F and 80°F. The higher the temperature within that range, the more quickly fermentation will happen. Avoid setting your jar next to electronic appliances, air vents, or other places that will expose it to temperature fluctuations throughout the day. Changes in temperature can activate different types of bacteria and negatively affect the flavor, so it's best to keep it somewhere as consistent as possible. If your home is on the cool side, wrapping your jars in towels or other thick fabric can help insulate them and keep them a bit warmer.

LIGHT

Acid-loving strains of bacteria do best in low light without any direct sun exposure. UV rays are effective at killing some types of bacteria and can affect your ferment's color, so it's best to eliminate that variable altogether. Ambient light is okay, but if your kitchen or fermentation station gets a lot of direct sun, it's best to tuck your ferments under a towel. No need to stick them in a dark pantry or closet—that's an easy way to forget them and come home to a sauerkraut explosion.

TIME

How long you leave your vegetables out to ferment at room temperature will have a significant impact on the texture, acidity level, and flavor of the final result. Generally speaking, the longer you leave your ferments out, the more sour they will become—but only up to a point. Once the bacteria have consumed all of the available sugars and starches in the vegetables, their activity dies down and the flavor levels out. Leaving your vegetables out beyond the recommended ranges provided in these recipes may result in a flavor you like even better; then again, a few extra days can mean the difference between deliciously sour and irredeemably rotten. That roll of the dice is part of the fun, and over time you'll develop a sense of what works best for you.

SALT AND WATER, WATER AND SALT

Other than the vegetables themselves, salt and water are the two most essential ingredients in lacto-fermentation. Here's what you should know about which kinds to use (and which to avoid).

Salt

Salt is an essential part of fermentation. When salt is added to vegetables, it helps firm up the pectin in their cell walls, promoting a crisp texture. Salt also inhibits the growth of bacteria that would otherwise cause the ferment to spoil, creating a window of time for the acid-loving bacteria to move in and get comfortable.

Each recipe in this book gives measurements in tablespoons, as opposed to grams. While it's more accurate to measure salt by weight using a kitchen scale, I know that many folks zone out when they see recipes calling for weighing and calculating. My goal here is to keep things as approachable as possible while still providing a reasonable range of accuracy. Consider the salt ratios as a good starting point from which to experiment.

The type of salt that you use also matters greatly in fermentation. The most practical choice is pickling salt, which is simply a fine grain table salt without any additives; sea salt with added minerals is great, too, but consider it extra credit. Kosher salt would fit the bill, but its big fluffy flakes give it less density—in other words, a tablespoon of kosher salt is less salt by weight than a tablespoon of pickling or sea salt.

> **HOW MUCH SALT IS TOO MUCH SALT?**
>
> Some people mistakenly believe that if salt helps keep things safe, adding even *more* salt will make things safer. In fact, salt is only needed at about 1 percent of the total vegetable weight. In other words, 16 ounces of vegetables only require 0.16 ounces of salt. Most ferments do best within a range of 2 to 3 percent, with cucumbers and some other watery, delicate veggies requiring higher salt concentrations to do their best.

Water

The antibacterial chemicals used to kill off harmful bacteria in our municipal water supply can also kill the very microbes we want to invite to the fermentation jar. The old method of boiling water to remove chlorine doesn't cut it anymore, as most municipal water is now treated with chloramine (chlorine combined with ammonia), which can't be boiled or evaporated off and isn't removed by the regular charcoal filters commonly used in homes. For the most consistent results, it's best to use distilled water, or water that's been filtered by reverse osmosis.

That said, in my personal fermentation practice, I frequently use tap water. I know that my local water supply here in San Francisco contains chloramine, but I do a lot of fermenting and prefer not to purchase plastic jugs of water if I can help it. I have never had a problem with a ferment that I could attribute to the water alone. My advice would be to start with distilled or filtered water and experiment with tap water once you've got the hang of things to see if you notice a significant difference.

A SAFE FERMENT IS A HAPPY FERMENT

One of the most common reasons people give for wanting to take my pickling classes is to learn how to ferment "without getting myself sick or poisoning anyone." I'm grateful that this common fear brings me good business, but I also see it as an indication of how our cultural fear of bacteria has made us lose our senses—literally.

When a ferment has gone bad, it's usually not shy about it. Smells that are putrid instead of tantalizingly sour, fuzzy molds that bloom from the top of the jar, and odd colors that appear in air pockets are all signs that something has skipped over sour and gone right into spoilage. Your body co-evolved with microbes; as such, it generally has a good way of guiding us toward good foods and away from harmful ones.

All of which is to say: If it's truly unsafe to eat, you'll know. If that doesn't reassure you, consider the fact that there are no documented cases of someone becoming sick from consuming properly fermented foods. Armed with the right techniques and your five senses, you can ferment with freedom.

FERMENTED VEGETABLE STORAGE 101

While I've given specific storage instructions and time frames for each recipe in this book, here are some general guidelines to keep in mind when storing your fermented vegetables for optimal freshness.

1. Store vegetables in the smallest jar that will fit your ferment. Avoid leaving half-empty jars, as this will allow more air to interact with the ferment, possibly causing oxidation or spoilage.

2. Avoid letting bits of the ferment hang out on the sides of the jars, especially those little shredded bits of kraut. After serving, press the vegetables back down to a uniform level.

3. Always use clean utensils to remove ferments from jars. Fingers and dirty tools can introduce new bacteria to the mix, potentially disrupting the ecosystem.

HOW TO STORE YOUR FERMENTS LIKE IT'S 1899

If you're tight on refrigerator space, you can try storing your ferment in a cool place like a basement, garage, or root cellar. As long as it has gone through proper acidification during the fermentation phase, it will be fine to store it at temperatures up to about 65°F, refrigerated or not. If you go this route, be aware that the ferment will likely get softer and sour more quickly than it would in the refrigerator.

CHAPTER THREE

LEARNING TO LACTO-FERMENT

In this chapter, I'll walk you through the two main methods of lacto-fermenting vegetables: dry-salting and brining. For the former, you'll follow a step-by-step tutorial to make a classic sauerkraut; for the latter, you'll do the same for pickles. Once you've learned these basic techniques, you'll be prepared to tackle all of the delicious vegetable ferments in the chapters that follow.

THE METHODS OF LACTO-FERMENTATION

As you know from chapter 1, lacto-fermentation is a magical microbial process. Take some vegetables, add some salt, keep them deprived of oxygen for a period of time, and bam: You've got tasty, probiotic-packed fermented food.

Unlike, say, kombucha, vegetables don't require a starter (a culture of specific bacteria introduced to achieve desired results) to kick off their fermentation process. They rely instead on their own bacteria and yeasts, which are plentiful enough to initiate fermentation on their own, given the right conditions. This process is called *wild*, or *spontaneous*, fermentation.

Now, to be fair, you may have seen recipes for fermenting vegetables that call for using a starter—typically whey or a bit of brine from a previous ferment. The idea behind using one of these starters to culture vegetables is that it can help nudge the fermentation process forward by adding a bit of the good bacteria—*Lactobacillus* and other acid-friendly strains—that we want to thrive in the ferment.

You can absolutely use a starter if that's your thing, and I've included a good resource in the Resources section (see page 137) if you wish to make your own whey. But I personally don't think it's necessary for the majority of vegetable ferments. Why add an extra step when wild fermentation yields such naturally delicious flavors on its own?

THE DRY-SALTING TUTORIAL: MAKING SAUERKRAUT

Dry-salting is the process used to make sauerkraut, some types of kimchi, and other ferments that call for finely shredding, grating, or slicing vegetables. For this method, salt is added directly to the vegetables, as opposed to being dissolved in water and then poured over veggies, as in the brining method that we'll cover later in the chapter.

While it makes sense to distinguish dry-salting from brining, the term itself is a bit of a misnomer: Once you start massaging that salt into the cabbage, for example, the result is anything but dry. All of that squeezing and crunching breaks down the cell walls of the cabbage, which helps the salt make its way in. As the salt enters the cabbage, it draws out the water stored in the cabbage's leaves via osmosis. Before long, you'll have a pool of liquid—or brine—to pack it in.

Cabbage, it should be noted, is a fermentation superstar. It contains a lot of extractable water to make brine, its cell walls are easily broken down by salt, and its sugars give the *Lactobacillus* and other desirable bacteria plenty to feed on. People figured this out a long time ago—as in, millennia ago. The word *sauerkraut* is German for "sour cabbage," but fermented cabbage is believed to have originated in northern China over 2,000 years ago before migrating along trade routes to Europe and beyond.

Sauerkraut is my go-to recipe when I'm teaching beginners to ferment. It's one of the simplest ferments to make, and it has endless flavor variations.

Let's use this classic sauerkraut recipe to learn the dry-salting process.

How *Not* to Mess Up Your First Sauerkraut

The process for making sauerkraut is simple: You shred cabbage, add salt, massage the mixture, season with spices as desired, pack it into a crock or jars, and wait for it to ferment. That's where the magic happens. But it's also where problems may arise. Fermentation is a forgiving process, but spoiled sauerkraut may be more common than you'd like at first. The exact cause for failure can remain a microbial mystery, though most of the issues that tend to occur when fermentation goes bad are preventable. Identifying specifically *how* it goes bad will help you troubleshoot and determine what to fix for next time.

This table covers potential blunders and the ways to prevent them.

THE BLUNDER	HOW TO PREVENT IT
The cabbage doesn't release enough liquid to cover the resulting sauerkraut.	Add another sprinkle of salt, then massage or pound the cabbage until more brine is released. Alternatively, top off the liquid with a saltwater solution of ½ tablespoon of salt to 1 cup of water.
The sauerkraut turns out slimy.	Ferment at cooler temperatures, and/or ferment for a shorter period of time (5 days), then move to the refrigerator; make sure all sauerkraut stays below the brine at all times.
There is a thin layer of white scum on top.	Use an air lock or skim daily to remove yeast buildup (this is usually harmless, but the result may taste off).
Sauerkraut is too soft in texture.	Increase the salt ratio in your next batch.
Sauerkraut grows mold on top layer.	Keep cabbage below the brine at all times, use an air lock, and/or fill jar within 1-inch of the top so that air can't allow mold to grow.

CLASSIC SAUERKRAUT

YIELD: MAKES ABOUT ½ GALLON

Prep time: 30 minutes • Fermentation period: 5 days to 2 weeks • Storage: Refrigerate for up to 1 year

FERMENTATION VESSEL

1 half-gallon jar

EQUIPMENT

Cutting board

Muddler, wooden spoon, or pounder

Large bowl

Large sharp knife or mandoline

Latex gloves (optional)

Fermentation weight (optional)

INGREDIENTS

1 large head green cabbage (about 3 pounds)

1 to 1½ tablespoons sea salt or pickling salt

1. Remove the outer leaves from the cabbage, reserving one or two for later. Use a sharp knife to halve the cabbage and then quarter it, removing and reserving the core pieces.

2. Use the knife or a mandoline to slice the cabbage into thin shreds about ⅛ inch thick, adding it to a large bowl as you go.

3. Sprinkle the salt evenly over the shredded cabbage, then massage it in with your hands, using gloves if desired, to release the juice. If you encounter any big rib pieces, simply break them up with your hands. A little texture variation is good, though, so don't worry if it's not all completely uniform.

4. After a few minutes of massaging, you should see liquid start to pool in the bottom of the bowl. If it doesn't, add another ½ tablespoon of salt. Now, you can choose to either continue massaging the cabbage to extract more juice or let it rest for 20 to 30 minutes, during which time more juice will naturally be released.

continued >

5. Pack the sauerkraut into a half-gallon jar by pressing it down firmly with a muddler or pounder. Pack it tightly, pushing out as many air bubbles as possible. As you pack, you should see the liquid rising up to almost cover the sauerkraut. Keep packing and pour in the collected liquid in the bowl until the sauerkraut is completely covered in brine. Leave at least 2 inches of headspace at the top of the jar for carbon dioxide expansion during fermentation.

6. Cover the top of the sauerkraut with one of the reserved cabbage leaves and weigh it down with the core pieces to keep it in place. Alternatively, you can use a fermentation weight or shot glass (as pictured). Again, make sure all the sauerkraut is completely below the brine—otherwise, it will attract bacteria and yeast from the air, potentially causing it to spoil.

7. Loosely place the lid on the jar to allow gases to escape during fermentation, or simply cover it with a clean towel to keep bugs and debris from finding their way in. Put the jar on a plate (to catch any overspill), out of direct sunlight and away from drafts. A temperature between 65°F and 80°F is ideal. Allow to ferment for 5 days to 2 weeks, tasting every day or two to see how the flavor is developing. Always ensure that the sauerkraut goes back below the brine after you taste.

8. Once it's sour enough to suit you, transfer the jar to the refrigerator, or pack the sauerkraut into smaller jars to refrigerate. This sauerkraut will keep in the refrigerator for a year or so, but it will become more sour and softer in texture over time.

THE BRINING TUTORIAL: MAKING PICKLES

Generally, brining is the method we use to ferment vegetables that are kept whole or in large pieces. Rather than massaging salt directly into the vegetables, salt is dissolved into water and then poured over whatever veggies we want to ferment. This is how we achieve the classic pickled cucumber, although as you'll see in chapter 5 (see page 57), the brining method is suitable for all types of vegetables. By adding saltwater and submerging the vegetables under the brine in a jar or crock, we create the necessary conditions to keep the microbes happy in their anaerobic environment.

This recipe for Classic Dill Pickles will teach you the brining basics. Once you've mastered these, you'll be ready to ferment all sorts of vegetables—and even mix them together to create chutneys, salsas, and relishes, like those in chapter 7 (see page 93).

How *Not* to Mess Up Your First Pickle

For Eastern Europeans immigrating to America during the 19th century, the pickled cucumber served as both a totem of Old World nostalgia and an avenue for new business. Today, they're more ubiquitous than baked beans. While the term *pickle* can technically refer to any food that's been acidified as a means of preservation (see page 31), ask any American to select one from a lineup, and they'll all point to the cucumber.

Interestingly enough, though, the cucumber is one of the most finicky vegetables to ferment due to its short lifespan, delicate nature, and high water content. This chart will help you avoid common mistakes.

THE BLUNDER	HOW TO PREVENT IT
The pickles are shriveled.	Try to pickle cucumbers within 24 hours of harvest and/or consider decreasing the salt ratio next time.
The pickles are soft and slippery.	Use a bit more salt next time, ensure that cucumbers do not rise above the brine level, and do not ferment at temperatures above 75°F.
Pickles are hollow on the inside.	Use smaller cucumbers (larger ones are often over-watered), and make sure cucumbers are freshly picked.
Scum or mold grows on the surface.	Use a fermentation weight or air lock to prevent air exposure; skim off scum every day or two.
The pickles have a strong, too-bitter taste.	Taste raw cucumbers before pickling; if bitter, try to find a different source.
Pickles end up spotted or discolored.	Use filtered or distilled water to prevent discoloration from hard water; use whole spices, not ground.

YIELD: MAKES ABOUT ½ GALLON

Prep time: 20 minutes • Fermentation period: 3 to 10 days • Storage: Refrigerate for up to 1 month

Adding grape leaves or horseradish leaves to your pickles will provide extra crunch insurance. The tannins in these leaves (also found in oak leaves) help keep the cells in the cucumber crisp, making for a crunchier pickle.

FERMENTATION VESSEL

1 half-gallon jar

EQUIPMENT

Cutting board

Knife

Bowl or quart jar

Zip-top bag or fermentation weight

INGREDIENTS

10 to 15 pickling cucumbers, or enough to fill a half-gallon jar

2 tablespoons dill seed, or
1 tablespoon dill seed and
1 tablespoon caraway seed

5 sprigs dill

5 garlic cloves, lightly crushed

3 to 4 grape leaves or horseradish leaves (optional)

2 to 3 tablespoons sea salt or pickling salt (see chart on page 30)

1 quart unchlorinated water

1. Trim just the very tip of the pale white-yellow blossom end of the cucumber. If you can't tell which is the blossom end, trim both ends. Leave cucumbers whole if they will fit, or halve if necessary.

2. Place half of the dill seed, dill sprigs, garlic, and grape leaves (if using) in the bottom of a half-gallon jar. Pack the cucumbers in tightly to fill the jar. Be careful not to

smoosh them too much—this may result in soft spots. Tuck the remaining dill seed, fresh dill, and garlic in among the cucumbers. Leave at least 2 inches of headspace at the top so that the pickles can be submerged below the brine.

3. In a small bowl or another jar, dissolve the salt in the water until it clarifies, then pour the brine over the

cucumbers. If more water is needed to cover the cucumbers, mix up more brine according to the ratios in the chart (see page 30).

continued >

— continued —

4. If any cucumbers are bobbing up above the brine, weigh them down by using a fermentation weight, wedging in another cucumber piece in sideways so that creates a block inside the jar, or filling a zip-top bag with brine and placing it in the neck of the jar.

5. With the top placed on loosely to allow fermentation gases to escape, leave the jar at room temperature in a spot away from light and drafts. Your pantry shelf is usually a good spot.

6. After 2 or 3 days, you should begin to see bubbles forming and the brine becoming cloudy. If you see white foam or scum forming at the top, skim it off every day or two to keep things in balance. Taste the pickles after 3 days to check on the flavor, then continue to taste every day until the desired tangy/sour flavor is achieved.

7. Once they're to your liking, cap and refrigerate the jar. This will slow down the fermentation and keep the flavor stable. They will keep in your refrigerator for about 1 month.

Troubleshooting: This chart will help you more precisely determine the proper amount of salt to use, in order to achieve the desired taste.

SALT AMOUNT (PER QUART OF WATER)	FERMENTATION PERIOD	PICKLE RESULT
2 tablespoons	3 to 4 days	Half-sour
2½ tablespoons	4 to 6 days	Medium-sour
3 tablespoons	6 to 8 days	Full-sour

Quick Pickle It

All of the pickles in this book are lacto-fermented, by way of brining, to achieve their sour flavor, build probiotics, and extend their shelf life. However, while all fermented vegetables are pickled, not all pickles are fermented. Pickling is a general term used to describe preservation via acid, whether that's acetic acid (vinegar) or lactic acid (created during lacto-fermentation). Most of the pickles you see on the shelves at stores are vinegar-brined. This method is favored by commercial producers, because it is much more predictable and doesn't require close temperature control.

In vinegar pickling, sometimes referred to as *quick pickling*, vegetables or fruits are bathed in a solution of vinegar, water, salt, and spices. The acetic acid in the vinegar is strong enough to kill nearly all of the bacteria—the good and the bad. After their bath, vinegar pickles are usually heat-processed to make them shelf stable for longer storage—an additional step that will kill any of the remaining bacteria. For this reason, you should never heat-process fermented pickles, unless you want to kill all those good little microbes you worked so hard to cultivate.

Unlike fermentation, where the salt initially inhibits bacterial growth until the acid-loving bacteria can produce enough lactic acid to take over, vinegar pickling relies entirely on the acidity of the vinegar. The salt does some work, but usually the levels are not high enough to act as a preservative.

Word to the wise: If you see a recipe or a (supposedly) fermented product at the store that includes vinegar as a main ingredient, be wary. It probably isn't the real deal.

CHAPTER FOUR

KRAUT, KIMCHI, AND OTHER CABBAGE CREATIONS

Cabbage is a fermentation superstar, and in this chapter, you'll see how it can be used in kraut, kimchi, and other ferments that pay homage to this humble yet mighty cruciferous queen. You'll notice that the process for many of these recipes is quite similar: salt, shred, submerge, wait, and then taste. Once you've got the hang of it, feel free to add your own flavor variations to any of the recipes here. Generally speaking, spices and seasonings can be changed without affecting the overall success of the fermentation process.

< Sunset Sauerkraut (page 34)

SUNSET SAUERKRAUT

YIELD: MAKES ABOUT 1 QUART

Prep time: 45 minutes • Fermentation period: 5 days to 2 weeks • Storage: Refrigerate for up to 1 year

Carrot, golden beet, and turmeric give this sunny kraut its golden glow. This beautiful ferment will dress up a rice bowl, salad, or soup with a blend of veggies that packs a powerful punch of probiotics—plus lots of flavor, thanks to the black pepper, turmeric, and ginger that season it up.

FERMENTATION VESSEL
1 quart jar

INGREDIENTS

½ head green cabbage, shredded (outer leaves removed and reserved)

3 carrots, grated

1 golden beet, grated

2 tablespoons minced fresh turmeric, or 2 teaspoons ground turmeric

2 tablespoons minced fresh ginger

1 garlic clove, minced

1 teaspoon freshly ground black pepper

1 tablespoon pickling or sea salt, plus more as needed

1. In a large bowl, add the cabbage, carrots, beet, turmeric, ginger, garlic, and black pepper, tossing to combine. Sprinkle the salt evenly over all, then massage it in with your hands, using gloves if desired, to release the juice.

2. Keep massaging until you see lots of liquid pooling; alternatively, let it rest for 20 to 30 minutes to allow more juice to be released. Add a few more pinches of salt if it's looking dry, then massage some more.

3. Using a muddler or pounder, press the mixture down into a quart jar, pushing out air bubbles as you go, until the brine rises up to almost cover the cabbage.

4. Top with any remaining liquid from the bowl, making sure everything is completely covered in brine. Leave at least 2 inches of headspace. Use the reserved cabbage leaves (or fermentation weight of your choice) to weigh the sauerkraut down. If any bits of vegetable continue to float up above the brine, push them back down below the cabbage leaf or remove them from the jar.

5. Place the lid on the jar, then place the jar on a plate out of direct sunlight and away from drafts to ferment for 5 days to 2 weeks, tasting every few days to see how the flavor is developing.

6. Once it's sour enough to suit you, transfer the jar to the refrigerator and store for up to 1 year.

That's Cool: Curcumin, the compound found in turmeric, is prized for its anti-inflammatory and antioxidant properties. Unfortunately, it is poorly absorbed in the bloodstream on its own. Pairing it with black pepper increases its absorption by up to 2,000 percent, so always reach for the pepper when adding a pinch of turmeric.

DILL PICKLE KRAUT

YIELD: MAKES ABOUT ½ GALLON

Prep time: 30 minutes • Fermentation period: 5 days to 2 weeks • Storage: Refrigerate for up to 1 year

This recipe brings two fermentation classics together for a hybrid hit. It's important to use small cucumbers without too many seeds; if you can't find those, you can remove the seed bed from a regular cucumber and use the rest of it. I use my own McVicker's Perfect Pickle Mix (available on my website), but you can use a store-bought mix or make your own using the instructions below, which yields about 1 cup.

FERMENTATION VESSEL

1 half-gallon jar

FOR THE PICKLING SPICE MIX

¼ cup dill seed

¼ cup caraway seed

¼ cup mustard seed

2 tablespoons coriander seed

1 tablespoon black peppercorns

1 tablespoon red pepper flakes

1 teaspoon allspice berries

1 star anise, broken into pieces

FOR THE KRAUT

1 head green cabbage, shredded (outer leaves removed and reserved)

1 tablespoon pickling or sea salt, plus more as needed

1 cup finely chopped pickling or Persian cucumber, or 1 cup chopped seeded regular cucumber

2 bunches fresh dill, chopped

3 garlic cloves, minced

TO MAKE THE PICKLING SPICE MIX

In a small jar, combine the dill seed, caraway seed, mustard seed, coriander seed, peppercorns, red pepper flakes, allspice berries, and star anise, shaking well to distribute. Seal tightly and store leftover mix for up to 6 months.

TO MAKE THE KRAUT

1. Put the cabbage in a large bowl. Sprinkle the salt evenly over the cabbage, then massage it in with your hands, using gloves if desired, to release the juice.

2. Keep massaging until you see lots of liquid pooling; alternatively, let it rest for 20 to 30 minutes to allow more juice to be released. Add a few more pinches of salt if it's looking dry, then massage some more.

3. Add the cucumber, dill, garlic, and 1 tablespoon of pickling spice mix, tossing it all to combine the seasonings.

4. Using a muddler or a pounder, press the mixture down into a half-gallon jar, pushing out air bubbles as you go, until the brine rises up to almost cover the cabbage.

5. Top with any remaining liquid from the bowl until everything is completely covered in brine. Leave at least 2 inches of headspace. Use the reserved cabbage leaves (or fermentation weight of your choice) to weigh

the sauerkraut down. If any bits of vegetable continue to float up above the brine, push them back down below the cabbage leaf or remove them from the jar.

6. Place the lid on the jar, then place the jar on a plate out of direct sunlight and away from drafts to ferment for 5 days to 2 weeks, tasting every few days to see how the flavor is developing.

7. Once it's sour enough to suit you, transfer the jar to the refrigerator and store for up to 1 year.

Get Funky: For an even funkier flavor, use a fermented pickle or two from the Classic Dill Pickles recipe (see page 29) instead of the 1 cup of chopped cucumber. Pour in a splash of the brine while you're at it (a couple of tablespoons or so) to jumpstart this pickle party!

APPLE CIDER SAUERKRAUT

YIELD: MAKES ABOUT ½ GALLON

Prep time: 30 minutes • **Fermentation period: 5 days to 2 weeks** • **Storage: Refrigerate for up to 1 year**

I'm declaring this the new fall seasonal delight, and as a bonus, it's actually good for you. If you don't have the various spices on hand and don't want to spend the time and money to round them all up, you could substitute about 1 tablespoon of pumpkin pie spice mix. Serve this in a scooped-out gourd for peak fall feels.

FERMENTATION VESSEL

1 half-gallon jar

INGREDIENTS

1 large head green cabbage, shredded (outer leaves removed and reserved)

1½ to 2 tablespoons pickling or sea salt

2 tart, crunchy apples, cored and shredded

1 tablespoon grated fresh ginger

1 teaspoon ground cinnamon, divided

½ teaspoon ground cloves, divided

½ teaspoon ground allspice, divided

3 star anise, broken into pieces, divided

1 to 2 cups unfiltered apple cider (optional)

1. Put the cabbage in a large bowl. Sprinkle the salt evenly over the cabbage, then massage it in with your hands, using gloves if desired, to release the juice.

2. Keep massaging until you see lots of liquid pooling; alternatively, let it rest for 20 to 30 minutes to allow more juice to be released.

3. While the cabbage rests, shred the apples using a food processor or grater.

4. Combine the apples and ginger with the salted cabbage, tossing well to combine.

5. Add ½ teaspoon of cinnamon, ¼ teaspoon of cloves, ¼ teaspoon of allspice, and half of the star anise to the bottom of a half-gallon jar. Using a muddler or pounder, press the mixture down into the jar, pushing out air bubbles and layering in the rest of the spices as you go, until the brine rises up to almost cover the cabbage.

6. Cover the cabbage mixture with 2 reserved cabbage leaves. Top off with the apple cider (if using) until everything is below the brine. If not using apple cider, add liquid from the bowl until everything is submerged. Leave at least 2 inches of headspace.

7. Place the lid on the jar, then place the jar on a plate out of direct sunlight and away from drafts to ferment for 5 days to 2 weeks, tasting every few days to see how the flavor is developing.

8. Once it's sour enough to suit you, transfer the jar to the refrigerator and store for up to 1 year.

Make It a Meal: Use this ferment on top of a bratwurst or your favorite sausage stew, giving an update to the classic pork chops and applesauce pairing.

PHO KRAUT

YIELD: MAKES ABOUT 1½ QUARTS

Prep time: 45 minutes • **Fermentation period: 5 to 10 days** • **Storage: Refrigerate for up to 6 months**

Vietnamese cuisine is all about those fresh herbs—shiso (a.k.a. perilla), cilantro, basil, mint, and many others each play a particular role on the table. This kraut integrates these fresh herbs and pho spices with cabbage for a noodle-worthy topping. If you have an Asian supermarket nearby, many of them will sell premixed pho spices in small bags. But I prefer to make my own.

FERMENTATION VESSEL

1 half-gallon jar

FOR THE PHO SPICE MIX

10 black peppercorns

3 star anise

2 whole cloves

1 teaspoon fennel seed

1 teaspoon coriander seed

½ teaspoon ground cinnamon

FOR THE KRAUT

1 (2-pound) head green cabbage, shredded (outer leaves removed and reserved)

½ small red onion, thinly sliced

1 jalapeño, thinly sliced

3 garlic cloves, thinly sliced

¼ cup chopped fresh cilantro

¼ cup chopped fresh basil

¼ cup chopped fresh shiso

¼ cup chopped fresh mint

Juice and grated zest of 1 lime

1 tablespoon pickling or sea salt, plus more as needed

TO MAKE THE PHO SPICE MIX

In a small jar, combine the peppercorns, anise, cloves, fennel, coriander, and cinnamon, shaking well to distribute.

TO MAKE THE KRAUT

1. In a large bowl, add the cabbage, onion, jalapeño, garlic, cilantro, basil, shiso, mint, and lime juice and zest, mixing well. Add the pho spice mix, sprinkle the salt evenly over all, then massage it in with your hands, using gloves if desired, to release the juice.

2. Keep massaging until you see lots of liquid pooling; alternatively, let it rest for 20 to 30 minutes to allow more juice to be released. Add a few more pinches of salt if it's looking dry, then massage some more.

3. Using a muddler or a pounder, press the mixture down into a half-gallon jar, pushing out air bubbles as you go, until the brine rises up to almost cover the cabbage.

4. Top with any remaining liquid from the bowl until everything is completely covered in brine. Leave at least 2 inches of headspace. Use the reserved cabbage leaves (or fermentation weight of your choice) to weigh the sauerkraut down. If any bits of vegetable continue to float up above the brine, push them back down below the cabbage leaf or remove them from the jar.

5. Place the lid on the jar, then place the jar on a plate out of direct sunlight and away from drafts to ferment for 5 to 10 days, tasting every few days to see how the flavor is developing.

6. Once it's sour enough to suit you, transfer the jar to the refrigerator and store for up to 6 months.

Get Funky: If you have access to a Vietnamese market, or any Asian supermarket with a good fresh produce section, look for some of the harder-to-find herbs like rau răm (Vietnamese coriander), Thai basil, and more. Feel free to experiment with these herbs in addition to those in the recipe.

Kimchi Class Is Now in Session

Kimchi is the national dish of Korea, and it's also quite beloved beyond its borders. In my years of teaching fermentation, I have introduced plenty of skeptics to the delights of kimchi. Even for those who aren't sure about the smell, that original aversion is frequently replaced by intense cravings for kimchi.

This spicy condiment originated in Korea during the Three Kingdoms period (1st century BCE to the 7th century CE) and remains a mainstay in Korean culture to this day. So essential is it to the Korean diet that, when heavy rains and flooding destroyed much of Korea's cabbage crop in 2010, the government had to temporarily suspend import tariffs on cabbage to alleviate the mounting "kimchi crisis."

Gochugaru: The Not-So-Secret Ingredient

Gochugaru is the red chile that gives kimchi its signature color and spice. The flavor is sweet and smoky with some definite heat, though it's mild enough to add several tablespoons or even a cup to a batch of kimchi without making the result intolerably spicy.

Gochugaru is typically sold as a coarse powder made from ground chiles that have been dried and blended together. It's an essential part of most kimchi, though there are some that don't use it, such as baek (white) kimchi. You should be able to find gochugaru in most Asian groceries, regardless of whether they're specifically Korean. If all else fails, you could make a passable substitute by blending 1 part ground cayenne with 4 parts sweet paprika.

There are at least 200 officially recognized varieties of kimchi and endless variations on those that change by region and by family. In the United States and elsewhere outside of Korea, people are most familiar with the red-tinted version that incorporates cabbage, radish, scallions, ginger, and garlic. However, the word *kimchi* (meaning "salted vegetables") actually refers to any combination of vegetables that is lacto-fermented in a similar process.

And what is that process, exactly? In the traditional method, kimchi is made by first salting Napa cabbage, either whole or in large pieces, and then letting it sit for several hours while the salt is absorbed into the cabbage and its own moisture is drawn out via osmosis. This can be done by dry-salting the cabbage and then weighing it down to express the moisture or by soaking the cabbage in a strong saltwater brine solution (about 5 percent salinity, or 1 tablespoon of salt per 1 cup of water).

What's Water Kimchi?

Water kimchi is a broad category of kimchi that uses a different process. Rather than dry-salting or soaking the vegetables, large vegetable pieces are submerged in a brine that typically uses the same kimchi seasonings you recognize in the more common version (garlic, ginger, and gochugaru).

Once it's fermented, kimchi will last indefinitely in the refrigerator and is unlikely to spoil (as in, grow fuzzy molds), given the acidity, plus the antimicrobial properties of the garlic, ginger, and chile. That said, there may come a time when your kimchi has become too sour or too soft to eat on its own. If that's the case, you can still use it to make kimchi pancakes, kimchi fried rice, kimchi stew, or other variations of your own design. In chapter 9, you'll find a recipe for kimchi stew and a kimchi Bloody Mary.

CHEAT-CHI

YIELD: MAKES ABOUT 1 GALLON

Prep time: 1 hour • Fermentation period: 2 to 3 days • Storage: Refrigerate for up to 6 months

I call this kimchi my "cheat" chi because it skips a few of the steps involved in making traditional kimchi. No soaking, no rinsing, and just a couple days of fermentation. The flavor may not be as nuanced as a traditional kimchi recipe (see page 46), but it will hit all the right notes and get you enjoying kimchi with far less effort.

FERMENTATION VESSEL
1 gallon jar or 2 half-gallon jars

INGREDIENTS

2 to 3 heads Napa cabbage (about 4 pounds)

⅓ cup pickling or sea salt

6 to 8 garlic cloves, minced

1 (2-inch) piece fresh ginger, minced

½ cup gochugaru

2 to 3 tablespoons fish sauce (optional)

2 medium daikons, peeled and cut into thin half-moons

2 to 3 tart green apples, Asian pears, or a combination, cut into thin half-moons

1 bunch scallions, white and light green parts only, thinly sliced

1. Remove and discard the outer leaves from the cabbage. Quarter the cabbage lengthwise and remove and discard the core. Cut each quarter crosswise into 2-inch pieces, then mix the cabbage with the salt in a large glass or stainless steel bowl.

2. Wearing disposable gloves, use your hands to distribute the salt evenly and massage the cabbage for 5 minutes. Allow the cabbage to sit for 20 to 30 minutes, or until it wilts.

3. While the cabbage is wilting, combine the garlic, ginger, gochugaru, and fish sauce (if using) in a food processor or blender. Purée until it forms a smooth paste.

4. Pour the collected water from the cabbage into a liquid measuring cup or jar. Scrape the paste onto the drained cabbage. Wearing disposable gloves, spread the paste all over the cabbage, tossing to coat well. Add a little of the reserved cabbage liquid to moisten, if needed. Add the daikons, apples, and scallions to the cabbage mixture. Mix well to coat everything.

5. Using a muddler or pounder, press the mixture down into a 1 gallon jar or 2 half-gallon jars, pushing out air bubbles as you go, until the brine rises up to cover the cabbage. Add more reserved cabbage liquid as needed to cover. Leave at least 1 inch of headspace.

6. Wipe off the mouth of the jar, place the lid on the jar, then place the jar on a plate out of direct sunlight and away from drafts to ferment for 2 to 3 days, tasting after day 2 to see how the flavor is developing.

7. Once it's sour enough to suit you, transfer the jar to the refrigerator and store for up to 6 months.

___

Make It a Meal: When this kimchi (and others) becomes too sour or too soft to eat, you can still use it in soups or fried rice.

TRADITIONAL BAECHU-KIMCHI

YIELD: MAKES ½ TO 1 GALLON

Prep time: 1 hour, plus 6 to 8 hours soaking time • Fermentation period: 2 to 4 days
Storage: Refrigerate for up to 6 months

This baechu-kimchi recipe is adapted from the version published by Colorado State University's Master Food Preservers. I volunteer as a Master Food Preserver in San Francisco County, and we regularly teach this recipe at community demos and hands-on workshops. It's always a hit. I've changed the brining process to make it a bit simpler and adapted some of the ratios to my taste. Remember: The longer you store kimchi, the more sour it becomes.

FERMENTATION VESSEL

1 gallon jar, 2 half-gallon jars, or 1 large food-grade plastic container

INGREDIENTS

2 medium heads Napa cabbage (about 6 to 8 pounds)

1 cup pickling or sea salt

1 gallon cold unchlorinated water

2 tablespoons sweet rice flour

½ cup unchlorinated water, room temperature

5 to 10 garlic cloves, minced

1 (1-inch) piece fresh ginger, minced

½ to 1 cup gochugaru

1 teaspoon fish sauce (optional)

10 scallions, white and light green parts only, cut into thin matchsticks

1 medium daikon, cut into thin matchsticks

1 Asian pear, cut into thin matchsticks

1. Remove and discard the outer leaves from the cabbage. Quarter the cabbage lengthwise and remove and discard the cores. Chop each quarter into 2- to 3-inch-wide pieces.

2. Put the cabbage pieces in a large bowl or food-grade plastic container large enough to hold them all.

3. Dissolve the salt in the cold water to make the brine.

4. Pour the brine over the cabbage pieces, then swish them around to ensure that no air pockets remain between them. Use a large plate or a sealed gallon freezer bag filled with water to weigh down the cabbage pieces so they stay submerged during the soak.

5. Soak the cabbage pieces at room temperature for 6 to 8 hours.

6. Rinse the cabbage pieces and squeeze a few times to release excess water, then set in a colander to drain for 15 minutes.

7. Make a paste by combining the rice flour and water in a small saucepan over medium-high heat. Bring to a gentle boil, stirring constantly, until it thickens. Set the paste aside to cool.

8. Add the garlic, ginger, and gochugaru to the cooled paste. This will make a chunky paste. If you prefer a smooth paste, use an immersion blender or small food processor to purée it. Add the fish sauce (if using), stirring to combine.

9. Wearing disposable gloves or using very clean hands, mix the paste with the scallions, daikon, and pear in a large bowl.

10. Add the drained cabbage pieces to the bowl, using your hands to spread the paste evenly over the cabbage.

11. Using a muddler or pounder, press the mixture down into a gallon jar, two half-gallon jars, or a large food-grade plastic container, pushing out air bubbles as you go, until the container is about two-thirds full. This leaves enough headspace for the expansion that will happen during this active fermentation.

12. Tightly place the lid on the jar, then place the jar on a plate out of direct sunlight and away from drafts to ferment for 2 days before transferring to the refrigerator. Alternatively, transfer immediately to the refrigerator and ferment for 3 to 4 days.

13. Store, tightly packed in the container to minimize air exposure, for up to 6 months in the refrigerator.

YIELD: MAKES ½ GALLON

Prep time: 1 hour • Fermentation period: 1 week 2 days • Storage: Refrigerate for up to 1 month

This recipe was inspired by Chef Edward Lee's green tomato kimchi recipe in his excellent book *Smoke and Pickles*. I swapped out the daikon for carrot, added lemongrass, and made a few other changes to make it my own. The result is a bright, crunchy kimchi that ferments for just a couple of days. It's very mild and a good one for folks who don't like kimchi—at least not yet.

FERMENTATION VESSEL

1 half-gallon jar or 2 quart jars

FOR THE PASTE

1½ cups unchlorinated water

¼ cup sweet rice flour

3 tablespoons sugar

2 to 3 carrots, coarsely chopped

2 garlic cloves, coarsely chopped

1 lemongrass stalk, tender inner leaves only, coarsely chopped

1 (2-inch) piece fresh ginger, coarsely chopped

2 tablespoons gochugaru

2 tablespoons fish sauce

2 tablespoons rice vinegar

½ cup coarsely chopped cilantro (optional)

FOR THE KIMCHI

1 pound Brussels sprouts, shredded

2 pounds green tomatoes, chopped

⅓ cup kosher salt

TO MAKE THE PASTE

1. Combine the water, rice flour, and sugar in a small saucepan over medium-high heat. Bring to a simmer, stirring constantly, until it thickens and holds together when stirred, about 2 minutes. Remove from the heat and cool to room temperature. Pour the paste into a bowl.

2. Combine the carrots, garlic, lemongrass, ginger, gochugaru, fish sauce, and rice vinegar in a food processor, then pulse several times until it makes a chunky mixture. Alternatively, use a knife (and some elbow grease) to mince it all up.

3. Stir the vegetable mixture into the cooled paste, then add the cilantro (if using).

TO MAKE THE KIMCHI

1. In a large bowl, combine the Brussels sprouts and tomatoes, then sprinkle the salt over all. Toss well, then let rest for 30 to 45 minutes at room temperature.

2. Transfer the tomato mixture to a colander, then drain and rinse. Return the mixture to the original bowl.

3. Mix the paste in with the tomato mixture, tossing to coat well.

4. Using a muddler or pounder, press the mixture down into a half-gallon jar or two quart jars, pushing out air bubbles as you go. There should be some liquid rising up, but it will be fairly dry—this is okay for this recipe.

5. Place the lid on the jar, then place the jar on a plate out of direct sunlight and away from drafts to ferment for 2 days. Transfer to the refrigerator to continue fermenting for 1 week before eating. Store in the refrigerator for up to 1 month.

NABAK-KIMCHI

YIELD: MAKES ABOUT 1½ QUARTS

Prep time: 1 hour • Fermentation period: 1 to 2 days • Storage: Refrigerate for up to 1 month

Nabak-kimchi is a type of water kimchi that features square pieces of cabbage and daikon floating in a cool and refreshing brine that's tinted pink from the gochugaru. It's traditionally enjoyed in the hot summer months, like a cross between cold soup and kimchi. The name comes from the technique for cutting vegetables into tidy squares called *nabak-nabak*.

FERMENTATION VESSEL
1 half-gallon jar

INGREDIENTS

1 small head Napa cabbage

2 cups daikon, peeled

2 tablespoons pickling or sea salt, divided

1 teaspoon sugar

5 cups unchlorinated water

1 tablespoon gochugaru

3 garlic cloves, halved

3 scallions, white parts only, cut into 1-inch pieces

1 Asian pear, cut into half-moons

1 (1-inch) piece fresh ginger, cut lengthwise into 4 pieces

1 Fresno or other medium-heat red chile, cut diagonally into thin rings

1. Remove and discard the outer leaves from the cabbage, leaving only the white and pale green inner parts. Halve the cabbage, then remove the base so that the leaves separate. Cut the cabbage leaves into 1-inch squares. Keep them uniform by stacking a few leaves on top of each other, cutting them lengthwise, then cutting them into smaller squares. You should end up with 2 to 3 cups of cabbage squares.

2. Cut the daikon into squares to match the cabbage.

3. Combine the cabbage and daikon in a large bowl. Sprinkle 1 tablespoon of salt over the vegetables and let them rest for 30 minutes.

4. While the vegetables rest, make the brine by dissolving the remaining 1 tablespoon of salt and the sugar in the water. Add the gochugaru and let it rest for 15 minutes.

5. While the brine rests, combine the garlic, scallions, pear, ginger, and chile in a large bowl. These are your seasoning vegetables.

6. Squeeze out the liquid that has been released from the cabbage and daikon, but don't rinse them.

7. Combine the cabbage and daikon with the seasoning vegetables, mixing together well. Transfer the vegetables to a half-gallon jar.

8. Pour the brine through a piece of cheesecloth or fine mesh strainer to remove the gochugaru (this will leave it with just a light pink hue). Then pour the brine over the vegetables. There's no need to pack anything down in this recipe; the veggies can just float in the brine.

9. Tightly place the lid on the jar, then place the jar on a plate out of direct sunlight and away from drafts to ferment for 1 to 2 days.

10. Transfer the jar to the refrigerator and store for up to 1 month.

Troubleshooting: Keep the daikon pieces uniform by cutting the daikon into flat discs, then cutting through a few of the discs at a time.

YIELD: MAKES ABOUT ¾ TO 1 GALLON

Prep time: 45 minutes • **Fermentation period: 4 to 10 days** • **Storage: Refrigerate for up to 1 year**

Curtido is a cabbage-based slaw that originates in El Salvador. You may recognize it as the delicious stuff served on top of pupusas. It is traditionally made with green cabbage, but using one red cabbage and one green one will give it a beautiful magenta hue. This lacto-fermented adaptation gives it more depth (not to mention, nutrients) than the vinegar version used by most commercial establishments.

FERMENTATION VESSEL
2 half-gallon jars or 1 half-gallon and 1 quart jar

INGREDIENTS

1 small head green cabbage

1 small head red cabbage

3 garlic cloves, minced

1 carrot, shredded or cut into thin slices

1 medium white onion, shredded or cut into thin slices

1 tablespoon cumin seed

1 tablespoon red pepper flakes

1 tablespoon dried Mexican oregano

1 bay leaf, crumbled

2½ tablespoons pickling or sea salt

1. Remove and discard any blemished outer leaves from the green and red cabbages. Remove 1 healthy-looking leaf from each cabbage and set them aside. Halve each cabbage, then remove cores. Thinly slice the cabbages with a sharp knife or mandoline, then transfer to a large bowl.

2. Add the garlic, carrot, onion, cumin, red pepper flakes, oregano, and bay leaf. Toss to combine well.

3. Sprinkle the salt evenly over all, then massage it in with your hands, using gloves if desired, to release the juice and make it wilt, about 5 minutes. Let it rest for 30 minutes to allow more juice to be released.

4. Using a muddler or pounder, press the mixture down into the two half-gallon jars, pushing out air bubbles as you go, until the brine rises up to almost cover the curtido.

5. Top with any remaining liquid from the bowl, making sure everything is completely covered in brine. Leave at least 2 inches of headspace. Use the reserved cabbage leaves (or weight of your choice) to weigh the curtido down.

6. Place the lids on the jars, then place them on a plate out of direct sunlight and away from drafts to ferment for 4 to 10 days, checking daily to make sure the curtido is still submerged and tasting it after 4 days to see how the flavor is developing.

7. Once it's sour enough to suit you, transfer the jars to the refrigerator and store for up to 1 year.

Make It a Meal: The complex spice layers and beautiful color make this ferment a showstopping condiment. Use it with tacos and quesadillas, on a sausage instead of sauerkraut, or as a topping for soups and stews (and, of course, pupusas).

DAIKON CUBE KIMCHI

YIELD: MAKES ABOUT 1 QUART

Prep time: 45 minutes • Fermentation period: 2 days • Storage: Refrigerate for up to 1 month

There's nothing like that satisfying, crunchy-yet-juicy texture of daikon. This long, white radish has a slightly softer texture and milder flavor than red radishes, and its porous texture soaks up flavor beautifully. If you can't find daikon, you can use red radish for this, but it will be much sharper and significantly more pungent. Note that this ferment is best stored in a shallow container so that the pieces remain evenly coated.

FERMENTATION VESSEL
1 large bowl

INGREDIENTS

1 large firm daikon, peeled and cut into bite-size cubes

1½ tablespoons pickling or sea salt

3 tablespoons sugar

2 garlic cloves, minced

1 (1-inch) piece fresh ginger, minced

¼ cup gochugaru

2 tablespoons fish sauce

1. Toss the daikon with the salt and sugar in a large bowl, then let it rest for 30 minutes.

2. Drain and discard the collected liquid, either by using a colander or by carefully pouring it out.

3. Toss the daikon with the garlic, ginger, gochugaru, and fish sauce, then press the mixture down into the bowl using a muddler or pounder.

4. Loosely cover the bowl with a layer of plastic wrap, then top with a clean kitchen towel.

5. Place the bowl out of direct sunlight and away from drafts to ferment for 2 days, stirring the mixture and packing it down again after 1 day.

6. Transfer the kimchi to a shallow container in the refrigerator and store for up to 1 month.

YIELD: MAKES ABOUT 1½ QUARTS

Prep time: 30 minutes • **Fermentation period: 1 to 2 weeks** • **Storage: Refrigerate for up to 1 year**

Teaching pickling workshops for the past several years, I've had the fortune to meet many Persian Americans who tell me about their love for torshi (sour vinegar-brined pickles) and shoor (salty fermented pickles). Passed on to me by one of my students, this interesting cabbage recipe calls for brining, not dry-salting.

FERMENTATION VESSEL

1 quart jar, plus 1 pint jar as needed

INGREDIENTS

1 small head red cabbage

2 quarts unchlorinated water

7 tablespoons sea salt

½ cup white wine vinegar

5 garlic cloves, thinly sliced

3 bird's eye or other hot chiles, thinly sliced (optional)

1. Remove and discard any blemished outer leaves from the cabbage. Remove 2 large healthy-looking leaves and set them aside. Halve the cabbage, then remove the core. Chop into 2-by-½-inch strips. Set aside.

2. In a medium saucepan, combine the water, salt, and vinegar, mixing to combine. Bring to a boil over medium heat, then immediately remove from the heat and allow the brine to cool until it is hot but not scalding.

3. While the brine cools, toss together the chopped cabbage, garlic, and chiles (if using) in a large bowl.

4. Using a muddler or pounder, press the mixture down into a quart jar, pushing out air bubbles as you go. If you have excess, pack the rest into a pint jar.

5. Check the temperature of the hot brine. The heat will help soften the cabbage so the brine can penetrate it, but if it's scalding, it will kill the microbes.

6. Pour the hot brine over the cabbage mixture, leaving about 1 inch of headspace. Place the reserved cabbage leaves on top to keep everything tucked under the brine.

7. Place the lid on the jar, then place the jar on a plate out of direct sunlight and away from drafts to ferment for 1 to 2 weeks, tasting every few days to see how the flavor is developing.

8. Once it's sour enough to suit you, transfer the jar to the refrigerator and store for up to 1 year.

CHAPTER FIVE

BRINED VEGETABLES

Brining is the method most commonly associated with the classic cucumber pickle. As you'll see in this chapter, the brining method can be used with most any vegetable. In these recipes, vegetables are cut into large pieces or even kept whole. Since we're not shredding them, we don't get the same liquid release from the cell walls as we do when shredding cabbage for sauerkraut or kimchi. For that reason, a saltwater solution, or brine, is necessary to keep them in an anaerobic environment while they ferment.

< Sour Corn on the Cob (page 63)

EASY HALF-SOUR NEW YORK DELI PICKLES

YIELD: MAKES ABOUT 10 PICKLES

Prep time: 20 minutes • Fermentation period: 7 to 10 days • Storage: Refrigerate for up to 6 months

If the idea of leaving vegetables out to ferment at room temperature is still something you're getting used to, this is the pickle for you. These crunchy, bright green, half-sour pickles will take longer to ferment in the refrigerator (my sweet spot is about 10 days), but this way, you don't have to mess with a fermentation weight or monitor them daily on the countertop. The waiting is, without a doubt, the hardest part.

FERMENTATION VESSEL

1 half-gallon jar

FOR THE PICKLING SPICE MIX

¼ cup dill seed

¼ cup caraway seed

¼ cup mustard seed

2 tablespoons coriander seed

1 tablespoon black peppercorns

1 tablespoon red pepper flakes

1 teaspoon allspice berries

1 star anise, broken into pieces

FOR THE PICKLES

10 (3- to 4-inch) pickling cucumbers, or enough to fill a half-gallon jar

1 quart unchlorinated water

2½ tablespoons plus ½ teaspoon pickling or sea salt

5 sprigs dill

3 garlic cloves, crushed and coarsely chopped

3 to 4 grape leaves or horseradish leaves (optional)

1 jalapeño or other medium-heat chile, sliced (optional)

TO MAKE THE PICKLING SPICE MIX

In a small jar or container, combine the dill seed, caraway, mustard seed, coriander, peppercorns, red pepper flakes, allspice berries, and star anise, shaking well to distribute. This will make about 1 cup. Seal tightly and store leftover mix for up to 6 months.

TO MAKE THE PICKLES

1. Wash the cucumbers gently but thoroughly, scrubbing off any dirt. Trim just the very tip of the pale white-yellow blossom end. If you can't tell which is the blossom end, trim both ends. Using a bamboo skewer or other thin skewer, pierce each cucumber through lengthwise from one end to the next. This will help the brine soak in more uniformly.

2. In a clean half-gallon jar, combine the water and salt. Cap and shake the brine to dissolve the salt completely. Make sure none of the salt remains at the bottom and no salt particles are visible in the water.

3. Add 1½ tablespoons of the pickling spice mix to the brine. Then add the dill, garlic, grape leaves (if using), and jalapeño (if using), swirling to distribute the spices.

4. Add the cucumbers, doing your best to push them down below the brine. Some will float to the surface—this is okay for this recipe.

5. Place the lid on the jar, then place the jar in the refrigerator to ferment for 7 to 10 days, giving the jar a shake every day or two to redistribute the brine and spices.

6. Store in the refrigerator for up to 6 months.

CURRY CAULIFLOWER

YIELD: MAKES ABOUT 1½ QUARTS

Prep time: 20 minutes • Fermentation period: 5 to 7 days • Storage: Refrigerate for up to 6 months

This is a fermented adaptation of my prize-winning pickle, which took home a 2017 Good Food Award from the Good Food Foundation. It incorporates all the same spices but boasts more flavor from the fermentation process. I use these little fermented florets to punch up stir-fries, noodle bowls, and even egg salad. Cauliflower is packed with vitamins C and K, so it's a great way to add nutrients in a variety of different dishes. The turmeric is optional, but provides extra color and an earthy flavor.

FERMENTATION VESSEL
2 quart jars or 1 half-gallon jar

INGREDIENTS

1 head cauliflower, cored and cut into small florets

½ medium white onion, thinly sliced

2 garlic cloves, halved

2 dried bird's eye or other hot chiles

1 tablespoon cumin seed

1 tablespoon coriander seed

1 tablespoon curry powder

½ teaspoon ground turmeric (optional)

1 quart unchlorinated water

1½ tablespoons pickling or sea salt

1. Pack the cauliflower firmly into two quart jars or a half-gallon jar, layering in the onion, garlic, and chiles and sprinkling in the cumin, coriander, curry powder, and turmeric (if using) as you go.

2. In a clean jar, combine the water and salt. Cap and shake the brine to dissolve the salt completely. Make sure none of the salt remains at the bottom and no salt particles are visible in the water.

3. Pour the brine over the cauliflower, leaving at least 1 inch of headspace. Use a wedge of onion (or fermentation weight of your choice) to keep everything under the brine.

4. Loosely place the lids on the jars or cover them with a clean towel. Place the jars on a plate out of direct sunlight and away from drafts to ferment for 5 to 7 days, tasting on day 5 to see how the flavor is developing.

5. Once it's sour enough to suit you, tightly cap the jars, transfer them to the refrigerator, and store for up to 6 months.

ESCABECHE (TAQUERIA PICKLES)

YIELD: MAKES ABOUT 2 QUARTS

Prep time: 30 minutes • Fermentation period: 5 to 7 days • Storage: Refrigerate for up to 1 year

Escabeche is that deliciously spicy mix of pickled vegetables frequently found on the salsa bar at taquerias. I've lived in California for 17 years, so I was pleasantly surprised to discover the best escabeche of my life on a trip home to my birthplace of Dodge City, Kansas—Tacos Jalisco on Wyatt Earp Boulevard, I salute you! This is my attempt to re-create their escabeche, only fermented instead of vinegar-brined.

FERMENTATION VESSEL
2 quart jars or 1 half-gallon jar

INGREDIENTS

2 pounds carrots, peeled and cut diagonally into ½-inch slices

8 garlic cloves, thinly sliced

4 jalapeño or serrano chiles, cut into ½-inch rings (seed for less heat)

1 medium white onion, cut into ½-inch slices

½ head cauliflower, cored and cut into bite-size florets

Juice and grated zest of 2 limes

4 bay leaves

2 teaspoons dried Mexican or regular oregano

2 teaspoons cumin seed

2 teaspoons black peppercorns, lightly crushed

6 cups unchlorinated water

2½ tablespoons pickling or sea salt

1. In a large bowl, combine the carrots, garlic, jalapeños, onion, cauliflower, lime juice and zest, bay leaves, oregano, cumin, and peppercorns, mixing and tossing to distribute the spices evenly.

2. Pack the veggies firmly into two quart jars or a half-gallon jar. If any spices remain in the bowl, scoop them out and add to the jars.

3. In a clean jar, combine the water and salt. Cap and shake the brine to dissolve the salt completely. Make sure none of the salt remains at the bottom and no salt particles are visible in the water.

4. Pour the brine over the veggies, leaving at least 1 inch of headspace. Use a wedge of onion (or fermentation weight of your choice) to keep everything under the brine.

5. Loosely place the lids on the jars or cover them with a clean towel. Place the jars on a plate out of direct sunlight and away from drafts to ferment for 5 to 7 days, tasting on day 5 to see how the flavor is developing.

6. Once it's sour enough to suit you, tightly cap the jars, transfer them to the refrigerator, and store for up to 1 year.

Get Funky: Add a drizzle of extra-virgin olive oil on top before serving these to get it a little closer to the real thing.

RED ONION RINGS

Prep time: 15 minutes • Fermentation period: 5 to 7 days • Storage: Refrigerate for up to 6 months

This recipe is as simple as it gets. Slice up some onions, add some herbs and spices, cover it with brine, and wait patiently for a few days while the sharp pungency of the onions gives way to a smoother, sourer flavor. I use these on burgers, tacos, pulled pork sliders, kale salads, rice bowls, chicken salad, and more.

FERMENTATION VESSEL

1 quart jar

INGREDIENTS

2 large red onions, cut into thin rings

2 sprigs thyme, oregano, or rosemary (optional)

1 teaspoon black peppercorns, crushed (optional)

2 cups unchlorinated water

1 tablespoon pickling or sea salt

1. Pack the onions firmly into a quart jar, layering in the thyme (if using) and peppercorns (if using) as you go.

2. In a clean jar, combine the water and salt. Cap and shake the brine to dissolve the salt completely. Make sure none of the salt remains at the bottom and no salt particles are visible in the water.

3. Pour the brine over the onions, leaving at least 1 inch of headspace. Use a wedge of onion (or fermentation weight of your choice) to keep everything under the brine.

4. Loosely place the lid on the jar or cover with a clean towel. Place the jar on a plate out of direct sunlight and away from drafts to ferment for 5 to 7 days, tasting on day 5 to see how the flavor is developing.

5. Once it's sour enough to suit you, tightly cap the jar, transfer it to the refrigerator, and store for up to 6 months.

Get Funky: Add a bay leaf or 1 teaspoon of cumin seed or red pepper flakes to spice things up a bit.

SOUR CORN ON THE COB

YIELD: MAKES 5 TO 10 CORNCOBS

Preparation time: 30 minutes • Fermentation time: 1 week • Storage: Refrigerate for up to 2 months

I had always assumed corn would be difficult to ferment because of the starches and sugars, so I was thrilled to discover that it works very well as a short-term ferment. The fermentation process sours the naturally sweet corn while softening the texture a bit, just enough to create a tender give before that satisfying tear from the cob.

FERMENTATION VESSEL
1 gallon jar or crock

INGREDIENTS

5 to 10 corncobs, husks and silks removed

3¾ to 7½ tablespoons pickling or sea salt (¾ tablespoon for each corncob used)

Unchlorinated water, as needed, to cover corncobs

5 to 10 garlic cloves, halved (1 for each corncob)

3 jalapeños, sliced, seeded, and membranes removed

1 tablespoon cumin seed

½ cup coarsely chopped cilantro stems

1. Bring a large pot of water to a boil over medium-high heat, then add the corncobs and blanch for about 30 seconds. This is just enough time to soften the cell walls and break down the starches a bit. Transfer the corn to a clean work surface or the refrigerator to cool.

2. In a gallon jar or crock, add the salt, then fill it halfway with water, swirling or capping and shaking to dissolve completely. Add the garlic, jalapeños, cumin, and cilantro.

3. Add the cooled corncobs to the jar. If the jar is large enough, add them whole. Otherwise, halve them before adding.

4. If necessary, add enough water to submerge the corn, leaving at least 2 inches of headspace. Add a small plate (or fermentation weight of your choice) to keep everything below the brine.

5. Loosely place the lid on the jar, then place the jar on a plate out of direct sunlight and away from drafts to ferment for up to 1 week, tasting every couple days to see how the flavor is developing.

6. Once it's sour enough to suit you, tightly cap the jar, transfer it to the refrigerator, and store for up to 2 months.

Make It a Meal: Grill these cobs just as you would fresh corn, then top with queso fresco, chopped cilantro, a squeeze of lime juice, and a sprinkle of ground chipotle for a Mexican street corn delight.

HORSERADISH BEETS

YIELD: MAKES ABOUT 1½ PINTS

Prep time: 20 minutes • Fermentation period: 7 to 10 days • Storage: Refrigerate for up to 6 months

Beets pair beautifully with horseradish, and their combined forces are delicious with ham or other salty meats. Flavor bombs aside, this recipe also favors your brain health. Beets are high in natural nitrates, which increase blood flow to the brain and may even help prevent certain types of dementia.

FERMENTATION VESSEL
1 quart jar

INGREDIENTS

2 medium beets, peeled and cut into thin matchsticks

2 carrots, peeled and cut into thin matchsticks

2 tablespoons grated fresh horseradish

1 tablespoon caraway seed

2 cups unchlorinated water

1 tablespoon pickling or sea salt

1. In a large bowl, combine the beets, carrots, horseradish, and caraway, mixing well.

2. Pack the veggies firmly into a quart jar. If any spices remain in the bowl, scoop them out and add to the jar.

3. In a clean jar, combine the water and salt. Cap and shake the brine to dissolve the salt completely. Make sure none of the salt remains at the bottom and no salt particles are visible in the water.

4. Pour the brine over the veggies, leaving at least 2 inches of headspace. Use a fermentation weight or air lock to press the veggies down, pushing down any veggies that bob up to the surface.

5. Place the lid on the jar, then place the jar on a plate out of direct sunlight and away from drafts to ferment for 7 to 10 days, or until the active bubbling stops, tasting on day 7 to see how the flavor is developing.

6. Once it's sour enough to suit you and the bubbles have stopped, tightly cap the jar, transfer it to the refrigerator, and store for up to 6 months.

Troubleshooting: If you'd rather not grate the horseradish yourself, use 3 tablespoons of prepared horseradish instead.

FERMENTED GREEN TOMATOES

YIELD: MAKES 1 QUART

Prep time: 30 minutes • **Fermentation period: 5 to 7 days** • **Storage: Refrigerate for up to 6 months**

Green tomatoes are easier to ferment than ripe red ones because they have less sugar and therefore won't ferment too quickly. This recipe is great for helping you make use of those end-of-season tomatoes that stay green on the vine. The spices in this recipe (celery seed, mustard seed, and allspice) give it a classic bread-and-butter pickle flavor, without the sugary sweetness.

FERMENTATION VESSEL
1 quart jar

INGREDIENTS

1 pound green tomatoes, cut into wedges

½ cup sliced white onion

2 teaspoons mustard seed

1 teaspoon celery seed

1 teaspoon black peppercorns, crushed

2 allspice berries

1 to 2 small dried Thai chiles (optional)

4 cups unchlorinated water

2 tablespoons pickling or sea salt

1. Pack the tomatoes into a quart jar, layering in the onion as you go.

2. Add the mustard seed, celery seed, peppercorns, allspice, and chiles (if using). Shake the jar gently to distribute the spices.

3. In a clean jar, combine the water and salt. Cap and shake the brine to dissolve the salt completely. Make sure none of the salt remains at the bottom and no salt particles are visible in the water.

4. Pour the brine over the veggies, leaving at least 2 inches of headspace. Reserve extra brine for later. Use a wedge of tomato (or fermentation weight of your choice) to keep everything under the brine.

continued >

— continued —

5. Loosely place the lid on the jar, then place the jar on a plate out of direct sunlight and away from drafts to ferment for 5 to 7 days, checking the jar each day to make sure everything has stayed under the brine. Remove any tomatoes that have bobbed up above the brine for a significant period of time. If the liquid level drops below the veggies, use the reserved brine to top it off. Taste on day 5 to see how the flavor is developing.

6. Once it's sour enough to suit you, tightly cap the jar, transfer it to the refrigerator, and store for up to 6 months.

Make It a Meal: These go great with crab cakes. For extra decadence, batter them and make fried green tomatoes. Yes, the heat will destroy most of the probiotics. But they will be delicious!

BUTTERNUT SQUASH MISOZUKE

YIELD: MAKES 1 QUART

Prep time: 30 minutes • **Fermentation period: 2 to 12 hours** • **Storage: Refrigerate for up to 1 week**

Misozuke are a type of Japanese pickle, in which vegetables are coated in miso, then set out to rest for a few hours. The sweet butternut squash soaks up the salty, umami flavors of the miso fabulously. While technically the squash doesn't ferment much in this short period of time, the fermented miso adds flavor and extends the life of the squash for up to 1 week. These are meant to be salty, so they're best enjoyed with simple rice dishes and other mild flavors.

FERMENTATION VESSEL
1 gallon zip-top bag or 1 food-grade plastic container

INGREDIENTS

1 tablespoon pickling or sea salt

½ medium butternut squash (just over 1 pound)

1 cup unpasteurized white miso

2 tablespoons mirin

1 tablespoon gochugaru or other red pepper flakes, plus more for serving (optional)

1. Fill a pot large enough to fit the squash with water. Add the salt and bring to a boil over medium-high heat.

2. While the water heats, peel the squash, then halve lengthwise. Scoop out and discard the seeds and pulp. Cut the squash into ½-inch-thick slices. Be careful, as the dense squash can be difficult to slice.

3. When the water boils, add the squash and blanch for 1 minute, working in batches if needed.

4. Remove the squash from the water with tongs, a slotted spoon, or a mesh strainer. Immediately rinse the squash under cool running water or dip in an ice-water bath for a few seconds.

5. In a small bowl, mix the miso and mirin, stirring well to combine. Stir in the gochugaru (if using).

6. Spread a thin layer of the miso mixture on the bottom of a gallon zip-top bag or food-grade plastic container large enough to fit the squash. Use your hands or a spatula to coat the squash with the miso mixture and place in the bag. Add a layer of the miso mixture on top to cover, then close the bag.

continued >

— continued —

7. Allow to sit at room temperature for 2 to 12 hours, tasting every 2 hours to see how the flavor is developing.

8. Once the flavor suits you, serve immediately or transfer to the refrigerator and store for up to 1 week. To serve, scrape off the miso and sprinkle additional gochugaru on top (if using).

CUMIN-PEPPER CARROT STICKS

YIELD: MAKES 1 QUART

Prep time: 30 minutes • Fermentation period: 5 to 7 days • Storage: Refrigerate for up to 6 months

Cumin-pepper carrots were one of the very first products I created and sold through McVicker Pickles. Something about the earthiness of cumin paired with the sweetness of the carrots and the sharp bite of the black pepper made this pickle an instant hit. Dip these fermented snack sticks in tahini or chop them up to use in soups and stews.

FERMENTATION VESSEL

1 quart jar

INGREDIENTS

1½ pounds rainbow or regular carrots, peeled

1 tablespoon cumin seed

1 tablespoon black peppercorns, lightly crushed

1 to 2 sprigs thyme (optional)

2 to 3 garlic cloves, peeled

1 quart unchlorinated water

2 tablespoons pickling or sea salt

1 teaspoon sugar

1. Cut the carrots into snack-size sticks to fit in a quart jar with about 2 inches of headspace.

2. Add the cumin, peppercorns, thyme (if using), and garlic to a quart jar. Pack the carrots firmly into the jar, being careful not to crush or break them.

3. In a clean jar, combine the water, salt, and sugar. Cap and shake the brine to dissolve the salt and sugar completely. Make sure none of the salt or sugar remains at the bottom and no particles are visible in the water.

4. Pour the brine over the carrots, leaving at least 1 inch of headspace. Use a piece of carrot (or fermentation weight of your choice) to keep everything under the brine.

5. Loosely place the lid on the jar, then place the jar on a plate out of direct sunlight and away from drafts to ferment for 5 to 7 days, tasting on day 2 to see how the flavor is developing. A harmless white scum may form on the top. Just skim it off every day or two to keep things in balance.

6. Once it's sour enough to suit you, tightly cap the jar, transfer it to the refrigerator, and store for up to 6 months.

Make It a Meal: Pour 1 can of black beans into a small saucepan over medium heat, and doctor it up with some spices. As the beans cook, chop up 2 or 3 fermented carrot sticks and toss them in. Drizzle a bit of brine on top and add a dollop of sour cream for a quick vegetarian lunch.

YIELD: MAKES ABOUT ½ GALLON

**Prep time: 45 minutes, plus 15 minutes to bake • Fermentation period: 3 to 7 days
Storage: Refrigerate for up to 6 months**

The word *torshi* means "sour" in Farsi, and this traditional Persian veggie medley is sour indeed. These are typically made with vinegar, but the layered flavors of vegetables, herbs, and spices come out beautifully when fermented. I adapted this recipe from Katrina Jazayeri's beautiful vinegar version featured in *The Immigrant Cookbook*. Dried limes can be found in Middle Eastern grocery stores or purchased online, although using the grated zest and juice from 1 lime is a solid compromise. You can serve this as a relish.

FERMENTATION VESSEL
1 half-gallon jar

INGREDIENTS

1 eggplant, peeled and cut into 1-inch cubes

½ tablespoon pickling or sea salt, plus 1½ tablespoons

4 garlic cloves, sliced

2 celery stalks, sliced

1 large carrot, peeled and finely chopped

1 medium cucumber, peeled and finely chopped

1 green bell pepper, finely chopped

1 dried lime, crushed

1 bird's eye chile

½ head cauliflower, cored and cut into small florets

½ cup chopped green cabbage

¼ cup finely chopped fresh parsley

¼ cup finely chopped fresh cilantro

¼ cup finely chopped fresh dill

1 teaspoon nigella seed

1 teaspoon fennel seed

1 teaspoon coriander seed

1 teaspoon ground turmeric

3 cups unchlorinated water

1. Preheat the oven to 350°F. Line a baking sheet with parchment paper or aluminum foil.

2. Season the eggplant with ½ tablespoon of the salt and place on the prepared baking sheet. Bake for 15 minutes, then remove and cool to room temperature.

3. In a large bowl, combine the baked eggplant, garlic, celery, carrot, cucumber, bell pepper, lime, chile, cauliflower, cabbage, parsley, cilantro, dill, nigella, fennel, coriander, and turmeric, mixing well.

4. Pack the eggplant mixture firmly into a half-gallon jar.

5. In a clean jar, combine the water and remaining 1½ tablespoons of salt. Cap and shake the brine to dissolve the salt completely. Make sure none of the salt remains at the bottom and no salt particles are visible in the water.

6. Pour the brine over the eggplant mixture, leaving at least 2 inches of headspace. Use a large piece of vegetable (or fermentation weight of your choice) to keep everything under the brine.

7. Place the lid on the jar, then place the jar on a plate out of direct sunlight and away from drafts to ferment for 3 to 7 days, tasting on day 3 to see how the flavor is developing.

8. Once it's sour enough to suit you, tightly cap the jar, transfer it to the refrigerator, and store for up to 6 months.

That's Cool: While the word *torshi* is Persian in origin, versions of this pickled condiment are common throughout the Middle East and Balkan regions. In these countries, it's still common for families and neighbors to come together in the fall to make torshi together over several days, preparing enough to last the whole year.

TURMERIC OKRA MASALA PICKLE

YIELD: MAKES 1 QUART

Prep time: 20 minutes • **Fermentation period: 5 to 14 days** • **Storage: Refrigerate for up to 6 months**

Technically speaking, okra isn't a vegetable—it's the seed pod of a flowering fruit in the mallow family, related to cotton and jute. But for this recipe, it's worth bending the rules! It's a fermented version of a product I created in collaboration with Sana Javeri Kadri, founder of Diaspora Co., who's on a mission to disrupt and decolonize the international spice trade.

FERMENTATION VESSEL

1 quart jar

INGREDIENTS

1 pound small okra pods

½ medium white onion, thinly sliced

1 tablespoon cumin seed

1 teaspoon smoked paprika

1 teaspoon Diaspora Co. ground turmeric, or ½ tablespoon grated fresh turmeric

1 small dried hot chile (optional)

1 quart unchlorinated water

2½ tablespoons pickling or sea salt

1. Gently clean the okra using a paper towel, clean cloth, or vegetable brush. Do not rinse or soak.

2. Combine the onion, cumin, paprika, and turmeric in a quart jar. Pack the okra firmly into the jar, being careful not to crush or break the pods. Slip in the chile (if using).

3. In a clean jar, combine the water and salt. Cap and shake the brine to dissolve the salt completely. Make sure none of the salt remains at the bottom and no salt particles are visible in the water.

4. Pour the brine over the okra, leaving at least 2 inches of headspace. Use a large piece of okra (or fermentation weight of your choice) to keep everything under the brine.

5. Loosely place the lid on the jar, then place the jar on a plate out of direct sunlight and away from drafts to ferment for 5 to 14 days, tasting on day 2 to see how the flavor is developing.

6. Once it's sour enough to suit you, tightly cap the jar, transfer it to the refrigerator, and store for up to 6 months.

Troubleshooting: Avoid rinsing okra pods too much or soaking them in water: The more moisture they're exposed to, the more the slime will come out. It's also important not to cut the pods; just trim the stem end if it's tough or brown. This will keep the glutinous part intact.

BEET KVASS

Prep time: 15 minutes • **Fermentation period: 4 to 10 days** • **Storage: Refrigerate for up to 1 month**

Kvass is a fermented beverage popular in Eastern Europe, typically fermented from leftover rye bread using the yeast. This is a beet-based version that's popular in Ukraine, and it's sort of a reverse pickle—it's the liquid you're going for here, not the veggies. I highly recommend using an air lock or burping the lid every day or so to release pressure, especially in warmer temperatures. Otherwise you'll have a beet soda fountain on your hands, which is just as messy as it sounds (speaking from experience, here).

FERMENTATION VESSEL
1 half-gallon jar or 2 quart jars

INGREDIENTS

4 to 5 medium beets
(about 3 pounds)

½ tablespoon pickling or sea salt

2 tablespoons sauerkraut brine or other brine (optional)

1 to 1½ quarts unchlorinated water

1. Wash and scrub the beets, but don't peel them. The microbes on the skin are beneficial to fermentation. Cut the beets into large chunks. Don't worry about keeping them uniform—you're just looking to expose the surfaces and help draw out the moisture a bit.

2. Pack the beets firmly into a half-gallon jar or two quart jars and sprinkle the salt over them. Add the sauerkraut brine (if using).

3. Add the water, covering the beets completely and leaving at least 2 inches of headspace. Cap and shake the jar to dissolve the salt completely. Make sure none of the salt remains at the bottom and no salt particles are visible in the water.

4. Tightly place the lid on the jar, then place the jar on a plate out of direct sunlight and away from drafts to ferment for 4 to 10 days, tasting on day 4 to see how the flavor is developing. A harmless white scum may form on the top. Just skim it off every day or two to keep things in balance.

continued >

BEET KVASS

— continued —

5. Once it's sour enough to suit you, strain, removing the beets. Serve the kvass immediately or bottle it in narrow-necked jars, seal tightly, and allow to ferment for another day or two at room temperature to build up more carbonation. Store in the refrigerator for up to 1 month.

Get Funky: Add 1 (2-inch) piece of ginger, coarsely chopped, to the jar when adding the beets to help slow down the fizz a bit (ginger is antimicrobial) and lend the kvass a bright ginger flavor.

KHIAR SHOOR (SALTY PERSIAN CUCUMBERS)

YIELD: MAKES 1 QUART

Prep time: 30 minutes • Fermentation period: 15 to 30 days • Storage: Refrigerate for up to 1 year

The term *khiar shoor* is Farsi for "salty cucumbers." These little gems are indeed saltier than your average pickle, intended to be eaten in small bites along with a meal or chopped up in a salad. As with many beloved, nostalgia-inducing foods, there is much debate about which herbs and spices should be included. But it's safe to say tarragon is essential.

FERMENTATION VESSEL
1 quart jar

INGREDIENTS

1 pound Persian cucumbers

4 sprigs tarragon

4 sprigs mint

3 garlic cloves, thinly sliced

2 dried red chiles (optional)

3 cups unchlorinated water

3 tablespoons pickling or sea salt

¼ cup apple cider vinegar

1 bay leaf

1. Wash the cucumbers well and trim off the stems if attached. Pat them dry with a clean towel.

2. Place 1 sprig of tarragon, 1 sprig of mint, the garlic, and chiles (if using) in a quart jar. Pack the cucumbers firmly in the jar, layering in the remaining tarragon and mint as you go. Take care not to press the cucumbers too tightly against each other—the brine needs to be able to circulate throughout the jar.

3. In a clean jar, combine the water and salt. Cap and shake the brine to dissolve the salt completely. Make sure none of the salt remains at the bottom and no salt particles are visible in the water.

4. Pour the brine over the cucumbers and add the vinegar, leaving 2 to 3 inches of headspace. Put the bay leaf on top of the brine. Use a large piece of cucumber (or fermentation weight of your choice) to keep everything under the brine.

continued >

5. Tightly place the lid on the jar, then place the jar on a plate out of direct sunlight and away from drafts to ferment for 15 to 30 days, tasting on day 15 to see how the flavor is developing.

6. Once it's sour enough to suit you, tightly cap the jar, transfer it to the refrigerator, and store for up to 1 year.

That's Cool: While khiar shoor are undeniably Persian, Persian cucumbers are not. This variety of sweet, smooth, and nearly seedless cucumber is believed to have originated on a kibbutz in Israel during the 1930s, then quickly spread throughout the Middle East. They're well suited to the climate and preferred for their flavor.

GINGER-GARLIC BEANS

YIELD: MAKES 1 QUART

Prep time: 30 minutes • Fermentation period: 3 to 5 days • Storage: Refrigerate for up to 6 months

Ginger and garlic are both naturally antimicrobial, so they help keep the "bad" funk in check. The good funk comes through quickly in this short ferment, which is ready in just a few days. I prefer the bright, still-fresh flavor of a shorter ferment for this recipe. Regardless, don't skimp on the ginger, as it really brings out the flavor and is a natural stomach soother.

FERMENTATION VESSEL

1 quart jar

INGREDIENTS

1 pound green beans, ends trimmed

5 to 6 thin slices fresh ginger, divided

2 garlic cloves, thinly sliced, divided

2 thin strips lemon zest, divided

1 teaspoon red pepper flakes, or 2 dried chiles, divided

3 cups unchlorinated water

1½ tablespoons pickling or sea salt

1. Make sure the beans fit into a quart jar with about 2 inches of headspace.

2. Place half of the ginger, garlic, lemon zest, and red pepper flakes in a quart jar. Pack the beans firmly into the jar, layering in the remaining half of the ginger, garlic, lemon zest, and red pepper flakes as you go.

3. In a clean jar, combine the water and salt. Cap and shake the brine to dissolve the salt completely. Make sure none of the salt remains at the bottom and no salt particles are visible in the water.

4. Pour the brine over the beans, leaving at least 2 inches of headspace. Use a large piece of carrot (or fermentation weight of your choice) to keep everything under the brine.

5. Loosely place the lid on the jar, then place the jar on a plate out of direct sunlight and away from drafts to ferment for 3 to 5 days, tasting on day 3 to see how the flavor is developing. A harmless white scum may form on the top. Just skim it off every day or two to keep things in balance.

6. Once it's sour enough to suit you, tightly cap the jar, transfer it to the refrigerator, and store for up to 6 months.

Get Funky: To make these classic dilly beans fit for the perfect Kimchi Mary (see page 125), switch out the ginger for 1 heaping tablespoon of dill seed and add a few dill sprigs.

PAO CAI (SICHUAN-STYLE FERMENTED VEGGIE MIX)

YIELD: MAKES ABOUT 1 QUART

Prep time: 30 minutes • Fermentation period: 2 to 5 days • Storage: Refrigerate for up to 1 week

In homes and restaurants across the Sichuan province of China, it's common to see bell-shaped glass crocks filled with fermenting veggies of all kinds. This quick ferment of mixed veggies is super easy to create, and it only needs to ferment for a couple of days. There is no set mixture of veggies: cabbage, green beans, carrots, cauliflower, bell pepper, radish—they all work. I like to make this when I've got a few random vegetables hanging out in my refrigerator that need a good home.

FERMENTATION VESSEL
1 quart jar

INGREDIENTS

3 cups unchlorinated water

1 tablespoon pickling or sea salt

1 tablespoon sugar

2 tablespoons clear liquor, such as gin or vodka

1 pound mixed veggies, cut into bite-size chunks

3 slices fresh ginger

2 dried chiles

2 star anise (optional)

1 teaspoon Sichuan peppercorns (optional)

1 large outer cabbage leaf

1. In a large bowl, combine the water, salt, and sugar, stirring until the salt and sugar are completely dissolved. Add the liquor.

2. Pack the assorted vegetables into a half-gallon jar, layering the ginger, chiles, star anise (if using), and peppercorns (if using), and mix well.

3. Pour the brine over the vegetables, leaving at least 2 inches of headspace. Tuck everything under the cabbage leaf and use the fermentation weight of your choice to keep everything under the brine.

4. Loosely place the lid on the jar, then place the jar on a plate out of direct sunlight and away from drafts to ferment for 2 to 5 days, tasting on day 2 to see how the flavor is developing.

5. Once it's sour enough to suit you, tightly cap the jar, transfer it to the refrigerator, and store for up to 1 week.

PICKLED MUSHROOMS WITH CELERY AND HERBS

Prep time: 20 minutes • Fermentation period: 7 to 10 days • Storage: Refrigerate for up to 2 months

Celery lends a bright vegetal flavor to the earthy mushrooms in this unique pickle combo. Once fermented, slice these up to mix into miso soup, noodles, or salads. And feel free to experiment with other fresh herbs, like parsley, tarragon, or oregano.

FERMENTATION VESSEL
1 quart jar

INGREDIENTS

½ pound large firm mushrooms, such as shiitake, cremini, or portobello, cleaned with a paper towel

3 to 4 celery stalks, cut into 1-inch pieces

1 shallot, thinly sliced

1 teaspoon chopped fresh rosemary

1 teaspoon chopped fresh thyme

5 black peppercorns, crushed

2 cups unchlorinated water

1 tablespoon pickling or sea salt

1. Pack the mushrooms, celery, shallot, rosemary, thyme, and peppercorns firmly to a quart jar.

2. In a clean jar, combine the water and salt. Cap and shake the brine to dissolve the salt completely. Make sure none of the salt remains at the bottom and no salt particles are visible in the water.

3. Pour the brine over the vegetables, leaving at least 1 inch of headspace. Use a piece of celery (or fermentation weight of your choice) to keep everything under the brine.

4. Tightly place the lid on the jar, then place the jar on a plate out of direct sunlight and away from drafts to ferment for 7 to 10 days, tasting on day 7 to see how the flavor is developing.

5. Once it's sour enough to suit you and the active bubbles stop, tightly cap the jar, transfer it to the refrigerator, and store for up to 2 months.

CHAPTER SIX

LEAFY GREENS

Leafy greens are some of the most nutrient-dense vegetables available. Their delicate nature make them a little tricky to ferment for long periods of time. For this reason, I find them better suited to shorter fermentation times, typically less than a week. The process is perfect for taking greens with a short shelf life and extending it a few days, or even a few weeks. Incorporating fermented leafy greens into soups and salads is a great way to access the nutrients embedded in their leaves without having to buy fresh greens every few days.

< Bok Choy and Watermelon Radish Kimchi (page 84)

SPICY MUSTARD GREENS

YIELD: MAKES ABOUT 3 QUARTS

Prep time: 30 minutes • **Fermentation period: 3 to 7 days** • **Storage: Refrigerate for up to 2 month**

I've long been a fan of Hawker Fare's incredible Thai–Lao flavor creations. So when the restaurant's namesake cookbook came out last year, I was thrilled to see that it included a recipe for their deliciously salty, sour, and slightly spicy fermented Chinese mustard greens, also called *dai gai choy*. The restaurant's version uses the starchy water from soaked white rice to help feed the ferment. Here, I've simplified it by using white sugar, which does the job just as well.

FERMENTATION VESSEL
1 gallon jar, food-grade plastic container, or large bowl

INGREDIENTS

2 pounds large Chinese mustard greens

8 garlic cloves, crushed

8 to 10 bird's eye chiles

2 tablespoons Sichuan peppercorns (optional)

2 quarts cold unchlorinated water

2½ tablespoons pickling or sea salt

2 tablespoons sugar

1. Remove and discard any blemished leaves from the outside of the greens. Cut the greens (including stems) into 3-inch-wide pieces. Wash well, then drain in a colander.

2. Pack the greens, garlic, chiles, and peppercorns (if using) firmly into a gallon jar, food-grade plastic container, or bowl large enough to hold it all. (I use a giant wooden salad bowl.)

3. In a large bowl or pot, combine the water, salt, and sugar, stirring to dissolve completely.

4. Pour the brine over the greens and cover the mixture with a layer of plastic wrap. Use as many pieces as needed to cover the greens completely.

5. Use a heavy plate (or fermentation weight of your choice) to keep everything under the brine. Finally, add another layer of plastic wrap on top of the container.

6. Place the container out of direct sunlight and away from drafts to ferment for 3 to 7 days, tasting on day 3 to see how the flavor is developing.

7. Once it's sour enough to suit you, transfer the container to the refrigerator and store for up to 2 months.

Make It a Meal: Try adding these greens to a stew, like the Sichuan Pork Noodle Soup (see page 129).

FERMENTED RAINBOW CHARD

YIELD: MAKES 1 QUART

Prep time: 15 minutes • Fermentation period: 3 to 7 days • Storage: Refrigerate for up to 1 month

Chard is packed with potassium, magnesium, vitamin A, vitamin C, and vitamin K—pretty much the whole alphabet. And as we know, these nutrients are further amplified by the fermentation process. Try adding this to bean soups, vegetarian barley stews, or stir-fries. Alternatively, if you really don't enjoy the texture of the fermented greens themselves, you can omit them and pickle the stalks only.

FERMENTATION VESSEL
1 quart jar

INGREDIENTS

1 bunch rainbow or Swiss chard

3 garlic cloves, thinly sliced

½ medium white or red onion, thinly sliced

1 tablespoon yellow mustard seed, lightly crushed

½ tablespoon pickling or sea salt

2 cups unchlorinated water, plus more as needed

1. Slice the green, leafy parts off the thick chard stalks and ribs. Trim the stalks and ribs so that they fit in a quart jar with about 1 inch of headspace. Chop the leaves into large pieces.

2. Pack the chard leaves and stems firmly into a quart jar, layering with the garlic and onion as you go. Add the mustard seed and salt.

3. Add the water, then cap the jar and shake to distribute evenly and dissolve the salt completely. Make sure none of the salt remains at the bottom and no salt particles are visible in the water.

4. Open the jar and add more water, if needed, to cover the chard and leave about 1 inch of headspace. Use a large piece of carrot (or fermentation weight of your choice) to keep everything under the brine.

5. Tightly place the lid on the jar, then place the jar on a plate out of direct sunlight and away from drafts to ferment for 3 to 7 days, tasting on day 3 to see how the flavor is developing.

6. Once it's sour enough to suit you, tightly cap the jar, transfer it to the refrigerator, and store for up to 1 month.

That's Cool: Although it's commonly referred to as Swiss chard, chard originates from the Mediterranean, not Switzerland.

BOK CHOY AND WATERMELON RADISH KIMCHI

YIELD: MAKES ABOUT 1½ QUARTS

Prep time: 45 minutes, plus 12 to 24 hours soaking time • Fermentation period: 3 to 7 days
Storage: Refrigerate for up to 2 months

Bok choy is a cruciferous cousin of cabbage, so it's great for making kimchi with extra crunch. Watermelon radishes get their name from the beautiful green, white, and pink colors revealed upon slicing them—no watermelon flavor, just a nice, radish bite. The colors will fade a bit during the brining process, but a pink hue will remain. This recipe is adapted from a version I found on the excellent preservation blog *Putting Up with Erin*.

FERMENTATION VESSEL
1 half-gallon jar or 2 quart jars

INGREDIENTS

2 pounds bok choy, cut into
1-inch pieces

1 carrot, peeled and grated

5 watermelon radishes, peeled and
cut into thin half-moons

8 cups unchlorinated water

3 tablespoons pickling or sea salt

3 tablespoons gochugaru

1 (1-inch) piece fresh ginger, minced

4 garlic cloves, minced

1. Combine the bok choy, carrot, and radishes in a large bowl.

2. In a clean jar, combine the water and salt. Cap and shake the brine to dissolve the salt completely. Make sure none of the salt remains at the bottom and no salt particles are visible in the water.

3. Pour the brine over the veggies. Use a large plate (or fermentation weight of your choice) to keep everything under the brine. Let soak for 12 to 24 hours.

4. Drain and reserve the brine from the veggies.

5. Wearing gloves, mix the gochugaru, ginger, and garlic into the veggies until everything is well coated.

6. Pack the boy choy mixture firmly into a half-gallon jar or two quart jars. Pour the brine over the vegetables to cover completely. Use a large piece of carrot (or fermentation weight of your choice) to keep everything under the brine.

7. Place the lid on the jar, then place the jar on a plate out of direct sunlight and away from drafts to ferment for 3 to 7 days, tasting on day 3 to see how the flavor is developing.

8. Once it's sour enough to suit you, tightly cap the jar, transfer it to the refrigerator, and store for up to 2 months.

That's Cool: Chow down on bok choy for nutrients galore! One cup of bok choy includes more than 100 percent of the recommended daily allowance of vitamin A, which helps promote healthy vision and strengthens immunity.

QUICK FERMENTED SPRING GREEN SALAD MIX

YIELD: MAKES ½ TO 1 QUART

Prep time: 15 minutes • Fermentation period: 3 to 4 days • Storage: Refrigerate for up to 1 month

Bump your salad game up a notch with this quick fermented spring salad mix. You can use any variety of fresh lettuce leaves you like (yes, even iceberg). To make it even simpler, you can make this with one of the premixed bags of spring salad greens you buy at the supermarket. Mix these in with fresh salad or add the bright greens to a rice bowl for a quick healthy meal.

FERMENTATION VESSEL

1 quart jar

INGREDIENTS

1 (5- to 8-ounce) bag spring salad mix or preferred lettuce

1 tablespoon pickling or sea salt, plus more as needed

Juice of 1 lemon

3 thin strips lemon zest

1 quart unchlorinated water, as needed

1. Rinse the salad mix, removing any wilted or brown leaves. Cut any large leaves into smaller pieces. Smaller leaves can be left whole.

2. Place the salad mix in a large bowl and sprinkle with 1 tablespoon of salt. Add the lemon juice and zest, then massage gently to work the salt into the leaves. Taste and add up to 1 tablespoon of additional salt as needed (you probably won't need that much).

3. Using a muddler or pounder, press the salad mix down into a quart jar, pushing out air bubbles as you go. It will likely only fill the jar about halfway. This is fine.

4. Use a sealed zip-top bag filled with water (or fermentation weight of your choice) to weigh the lettuce down. This should pull additional moisture from the lettuce as it sits.

5. Let the lettuce ferment at room temperature for 24 hours.

6. The lettuce should have released enough moisture to be sitting in its own brine. If not, in a clean jar, combine the water and 2 tablespoons of salt. Cap and shake the brine to dissolve the salt completely. Make sure none of the salt remains at the bottom and no salt particles are visible in the water. Pour the brine over the lettuce to cover, making sure everything is below the brine.

7. Place the lid on the jar, then place the jar on a plate out of direct sunlight and away from drafts to ferment for 2 to 3 days, tasting on day 2 to see how the flavor is developing.

8. Once it's sour enough to suit you, tightly cap the jar, transfer it to the refrigerator, and store for up to 1 month.

PICKLED LETTUCE HEADS

YIELD: MAKES ABOUT ½ GALLON

Prep time: 10 minutes • Fermentation period: 3 to 7 days • Storage: Refrigerate for up to 1 month

Soaking your lettuce may sound like a recipe for sogginess, but the brining technique works surprisingly well for a short ferment of baby romaine lettuce heads. You could also try this recipe with butterhead lettuce, Belgian endives, or any tender young lettuce. I like to use these as wrappers for spring rolls instead of rice paper, or as cups for serving salad. Alternatively, you can use them just like you would fresh lettuce in salads, mixing some fermented lettuce with fresh lettuce for texture and flavor variety.

FERMENTATION VESSEL
1 half-gallon jar

INGREDIENTS

6 baby romaine lettuce heads, or as many as you can easily fit in a half-gallon jar

6 garlic cloves, minced

1 bunch fresh dill

2 tablespoons minced fresh horseradish

1 quart unchlorinated water, plus more as needed

2 tablespoons pickling or sea salt, plus more as needed

1. Rinse the lettuce heads well, then shake off excess water and pat dry. Trim the cores, but do not remove them—you want to keep the heads all together in one piece.

2. Place the lettuce heads in the jar core-side up, layering the garlic, dill, and horseradish in between and around the heads.

3. In a clean jar, combine the water and salt. Cap and shake the brine to dissolve the salt completely. Make sure none of the salt remains at the bottom and no salt particles are visible in the water.

4. Pour the brine over the lettuce heads, leaving at least 2 inches of headspace. If more brine is needed to cover, mix 1 tablespoon of salt with 2 cups of unchlorinated water, then top it off until the lettuce heads are completely submerged. Use a large piece of vegetable (or fermentation weight of your choice) to keep everything under the brine.

5. Place the lid on the jar, then place the jar on a plate out of direct sunlight and away from drafts to ferment for 3 to 7 days, tasting on day 3 to see how the flavor is developing.

6. Once it's sour enough to suit you, tightly cap the jar, transfer it to the refrigerator, and store for up to 1 month.

SHISO LEAVES

Prep time: 15 minutes • Fermentation period: 10 to 15 days • Storage: Refrigerate for up to 6 months

Native to East Asia and Southeast Asia, shiso, also known as perilla, tastes like a cross between mint, basil, and sweet licorice, with a hint of citrus. And yet even with all those comparisons, it's hard to describe its unique flavor—you just have to experience it for yourself. With the salty and sour flavors imparted from the fermentation process, you'll have an incredibly flavorful and surprisingly versatile ferment to use in everything from salads to sushi. Depending on your location, you may find shiso at farmers' markets or Asian supermarkets.

FERMENTATION VESSEL
1 pint jar

INGREDIENTS

2 bunches red or green shiso leaves

½ teaspoon pickling or sea salt

1 tablespoon minced fresh ginger (optional)

1. Rinse the leaves well and cut or snap them from the stems so that just the whole leaf remains. Discard the stems.

2. Put the shiso leaves in a shallow bowl and sprinkle with the salt. Toss the salt and leaves together and massage gently—these tender leaves will start wilting almost right away. Mix in the ginger (if using). At this point, you should see a bit of liquid releasing from the leaves. (It won't release enough juice to create a brine, so don't worry if you don't see much liquid.)

3. Using a muddler or pounder, press the mixture down into a pint jar, pushing out air bubbles as you go. Use a sealed zip-top bag filled with water to weigh everything down.

4. Place the lid on the jar, then place the jar on a plate out of direct sunlight and away from drafts to ferment for 10 to 15 days, tasting on day 10 to see how the flavor is developing.

continued >

5. Once it's sour enough to suit you, tightly cap the jar, transfer it to the refrigerator, and store for up to 6 months.

That's Cool: In Chinese medicine, shiso is used to treat coughs and other respiratory ailments. Throughout Asia, the antioxidant and anti-inflammatory properties of the leaves make it popular as a tea, administered to help soothe allergies and strengthen the immune system.

CILANTRO LEAVES

Prep time: 20 minutes • Fermentation period: 10 to 15 days • Storage: Refrigerate for up to 6 months

You already know how you feel about cilantro, I'd imagine. If you're in the "tastes like soap" camp, I won't try to convince you. If you're a cilantro supporter, however, give this one a go. Cilantro is the leaf of the coriander plant, and the leaves and seeds have completely different but complementary flavors. So, why not reunite these two parts of the same plant in the fermentation jar?

FERMENTATION VESSEL
1 pint jar

INGREDIENTS

2 bunches fresh cilantro

½ teaspoon sea salt

1 tablespoon coriander seed

1. Use the tines of a fork to strip the cilantro leaves from their stems or pick them off by hand. Discard the stems or reserve for another use.

2. Put the leaves in a shallow bowl and sprinkle with the salt. Toss the salt and leaves together and massage gently—these tender leaves will start wilting almost right away. Mix in the coriander. At this point, you should see a bit of liquid releasing from the leaves. (It won't release enough juice to create a brine, so don't worry if you don't see much liquid.)

3. Using a muddler or pounder, press the mixture down into a pint jar, pushing out air bubbles as you go. Use a sealed zip-top bag filled with water to weigh everything down.

4. Place the lid on the jar, then place the jar on a plate out of direct sunlight and away from drafts to ferment for 10 to 15 days, tasting on day 10 to see how the flavor is developing.

5. Once it's sour enough to suit you, tightly cap the jar, transfer it to the refrigerator, and store for up to 6 months.

That's Cool: The coriander plant is one of the oldest and most widely used culinary herbs. Coriander seed has even been found in tombs of the ancient Egyptians.

CHAPTER SEVEN

CHUTNEYS, RELISHES, AND SALSAS

The recipes in this chapter all have one thing in common: They're chunky mixtures with a lot of flavor. Since they consist of vegetables (and, okay, *occasionally* fruits) chopped up in small bits, they present a bit more of a challenge in terms of keeping everything tucked under the brine. I'll give you some instructions on how to deal with this, but you'll want to keep a close eye on these ferments, regardless, to make sure air pockets don't develop. Using the smallest jar possible for your ferment will help prevent oxidation and yeast from developing on the surface.

< Haitian Pikliz (page 96)

ISRAELI SALAD

YIELD: MAKES 1 QUART

Prep time: 20 minutes • Fermentation period: 1 to 2 days • Storage: Refrigerate for up to 1 week

Versions of this fresh chopped salad appear throughout the Middle East. People put their own spin on it from region to region, but its core elements remain the same—cucumbers, tomato, onion, and parsley. The combined forces of these veggies create a salad packed with health benefits. This recipe employs the brining technique, so you don't have to do any pressing or waiting for the vegetables to make their own brine.

FERMENTATION VESSEL

1 quart jar

INGREDIENTS

1 pound Persian cucumbers, chopped

1 pound firm ripe tomatoes, seeded and chopped

½ cup minced fresh parsley

⅓ cup minced red onion

3 tablespoons freshly squeezed lemon juice

2 cups water

2 teaspoons sea salt

1. Combine the cucumbers, tomato, parsley, and onion in a large bowl. Add the lemon juice, tossing to combine evenly.

2. Pack the salad mixture firmly into a quart jar, pressing down to get rid of any air pockets.

3. In a clean jar, combine the water and salt. Cap and shake the brine to dissolve the salt completely. Make sure none of the salt remains at the bottom and no salt particles are visible in the water.

4. Pour the brine over the veggies until they're completely covered. You can use a fermentation weight to keep them down, but with the short fermentation time, it's not essential.

5. Tightly place the lid on the jar, then place the jar on a plate out of direct sunlight and away from drafts to ferment for 1 to 2 days, tasting on day 1 to see how the flavor is developing. This one shouldn't ferment longer than 2 days.

6. Serve right away at room temperature or transfer the jar to the refrigerator and store for up to 1 week.

That's Cool: Like many fixtures associated with Israeli national cuisine (hummus, tabbouleh), this salad originated as a dish enjoyed by Palestinian Arabs in the countryside. The term *Israeli salad* is primarily used outside of Israel. On Israeli menus, it's often called *salat aravi* (Arab salad) or *salat katzutz* (chopped salad).

CHILERO TICO

YIELD: MAKES 1 QUART

Prep time: 30 minutes • Fermentation period: 5 to 10 days • Storage: Refrigerate for up to 1 year

Somewhere between a pickle, a dressing, and a salsa, chilero can be found packed into glass bottles on most Costa Rican tables. Each region, or even each family, has its preferred blend, texture, and heat level. The deeply flavored brine picks up the seasonings of the thinly sliced veggies and spices, making it uniquely suited to livening up the mainstays of the generally mildly flavored Costa Rican diet.

FERMENTATION VESSEL
1 quart jar

INGREDIENTS

6 to 8 carrots, grated
(about 3 cups)

3 garlic cloves, minced

1 medium red onion, thinly sliced

1 medium green bell
pepper, chopped

1 jalapeño, chopped

Juice of 2 limes

1 teaspoon dried oregano

2 tablespoons pickling or sea salt

Unchlorinated water, as needed,
to cover veggies

1. Combine the carrots, garlic, onion, bell pepper, jalapeño, lime juice, and oregano in a large bowl. Add the salt and massage it in until liquid pools in the bottom of the bowl. Let it sit for 15 to 20 minutes, then massage some more to release more liquid from the veggies.

2. Using a muddler or pounder, press the mixture down into a quart jar, pushing out air bubbles as you go, until the brine rises up high as possible. Add enough water to cover the veggies by 1 to 2 inches.

3. Use a large piece of carrot (or fermentation weight of your choice) to keep everything under the brine.

4. Tightly place the lid on the jar, then place the jar on a plate out of direct sunlight and away from drafts to ferment for 5 to 10 days, tasting on day 5 to see how the flavor is developing. If you see pressure building up, burp the lid daily to release the gases. Alternatively, use an air lock on top of the jar.

5. Once it's sour enough to suit you, tightly cap the jar, transfer it to the refrigerator, and store for up to 1 year.

HAITIAN PIKLIZ

YIELD: MAKES ABOUT 1½ QUARTS

Prep time: 45 minutes • **Fermentation period: 7 to 10 days** • **Storage: Refrigerate for up to 1 year**

Pikliz is a spicy, cabbage-based Haitian condiment—sort of like a sauerkraut with the flavors dialed up to 11. The warm spices (clove and allspice) pair beautifully with the heat of the Scotch bonnet chiles. Plus, as you'll soon see for yourself, it goes well with everything. You can use the shredding blade on a food processor to make the shredding go faster, but the texture will be better if you take the time to do it by hand.

FERMENTATION VESSEL
1 quart jar, plus 1 pint jar as needed

INGREDIENTS

1 small head green cabbage, thinly sliced (outer leaves removed and reserved)

1 carrot, thinly sliced

1 red bell pepper, thinly sliced

1 small red or white onion, thinly sliced

2 Scotch bonnet chiles, minced

6 garlic cloves, minced

Juice of 2 limes

12 allspice berries

12 whole cloves

½ teaspoon dried thyme

1 tablespoon pickling or sea salt

1. Combine the cabbage, carrot, bell pepper, onion, chiles, garlic, lime juice, allspice, cloves, and thyme in a large bowl. Add the salt and massage it in until liquid pools in the bottom if the bowl.

2. Using a muddler or pounder, press the mixture down into a quart jar, pushing out air bubbles as you go, until the brine rises up high as possible. If you have more than a quart, pack the remaining pikliz into a pint jar.

3. Place the reserved cabbage leaves on top to keep the small bits from floating to the surface. Use a fermentation weight, if needed, to make sure everything stays below the brine.

4. Tightly place the lid on the jar, then place the jar on a plate out of direct sunlight and away from drafts to ferment for 7 to 10 days, tasting on day 7 to see how the flavor is developing. If you see pressure building up, burp the lid daily to release the gases. Alternatively, use an air lock on top of the jar.

5. Once it's sour enough to suit you, tightly cap the jar, transfer it to the refrigerator, and store for up to 1 year.

Make It a Meal: Pikliz is traditionally served with *griot*, a Haitian dish featuring cubed pork marinated in citrus juices, then simmered and fried. If that isn't in your wheelhouse, use pikliz with pulled pork sandwiches, pork tacos, or sliders.

BUTTERNUT CHUTNEY

YIELD: MAKES 1 QUART

Prep time: 15 minutes, plus 45 minutes rest time • Fermentation period: 1 to 3 weeks
Storage: Refrigerate for up to 1 year

Chutney is a bit of a diaspora dish, having originated on the Indian subcontinent and then spread worldwide, picking up influences that altered its flavor depending on the location. Featuring squash indigenous to the Americas, carrots that were originally cultivated in Persia, and of course, spices from India, this map-circling medley is as complex as it is delicious. You can use the shredding blade of a food processor to make the shredding easier.

FERMENTATION VESSEL

1 quart jar

INGREDIENTS

1½ pounds butternut squash, shredded

1 carrot, shredded

1 small onion, thinly sliced

3 garlic cloves, minced

½ cup raisins, chopped

½ teaspoon freshly ground cardamom

½ teaspoon turmeric

Pinch freshly ground black pepper

Pinch nutmeg

2 teaspoons pickling or sea salt

1. Combine the squash, carrot, onion, garlic, raisins, cardamom, turmeric, black pepper, and nutmeg in a large bowl. Add the salt and massage it in well. Cover the bowl loosely with a clean towel and let sit for 45 minutes, then massage a bit more, until liquid pools in the bottom of the bowl.

2. Using a muddler or pounder, press the mixture down into a quart jar, pushing out air bubbles as you go. Use a fermentation weight of your choice to make sure everything stays pressed down.

3. Tightly place the lid on the jar, then place the jar on a plate out of direct sunlight and away from drafts to ferment for 1 to 3 weeks, tasting after 1 week to see how the flavor is developing. If you see pressure building up, burp the lid daily to release the gases. Alternatively, use an air lock on top of the jar.

4. Once it's sour enough to suit you, tightly cap the jar, transfer it to the refrigerator, and store for up to 1 year.

Get Funky: Add 1 broken cinnamon stick, 3 cloves, and 3 allspice berries to spike this chutney with fall-forward flavor.

RHUBARB CHUTNEY

Prep time: 15 minutes • Fermentation period: 2 to 5 days • Storage: Refrigerate for up to 2 weeks

We tend to treat rhubarb like a fruit, sweetening it up and mixing it with strawberries for a jam or pie. But if you've ever tasted it raw and unsweetened, you may not be all that surprised to learn that rhubarb is actually a vegetable. This recipe takes it in a more savory direction, with just a bit of sweetness coming from the raisins. Try this as a pancake topping, spoon some into your granola and yogurt, or make it a unique addition to your next cheese plate.

FERMENTATION VESSEL
1 quart jar (wide mouth preferred)

INGREDIENTS

2 cups chopped rhubarb stalks (about 3 medium stalks)

½ cup coarsely chopped raisins

¼ cup chopped shelled pistachios

¼ cup chopped red onion

1 teaspoon pickling or sea salt

½ teaspoon ground cinnamon

½ teaspoon freshly ground black pepper

2 tablespoons brine from previous batch of sauerkraut or pickles (optional)

¾ cup unchlorinated water

1. Put the rhubarb in a quart jar. Add the raisins, pistachios, onion, salt, cinnamon, and black pepper. Add the brine (if using).

2. Pour the water over the rhubarb. Cap and shake the jar to dissolve the salt completely and mix the ingredients. Open the jar and use a fermentation weight of your choice to keep everything under the brine.

3. Tightly place the lid on the jar, then place the jar on a plate out of direct sunlight and away from drafts to ferment for 2 to 5 days, tasting on day 2 to see how the flavor is developing. Check daily to ensure that the liquid level is still covering the rhubarb.

4. Once it's bubbly and sour enough to suit you, tightly cap the jar, transfer it to the refrigerator, and store for up to 2 weeks.

That's Cool: Rhubarb leaves contain oxalic acid, a highly poisonous compound that can cause severe kidney damage if eaten in large quantities. Leave these leaves for the compost!

SPICY ONION-MANGO CHUTNEY

YIELD: MAKES ABOUT 1 PINT

Prep time: 30 minutes • Fermentation period: 10 to 14 days • Storage: Refrigerate for up to 1 year

This recipe is adapted from a version found in Kirsten and Christopher Shockey's wonderful book, *Fiery Ferments*. It's great to make in the winter when you want something special to brighten up your meals and there's not a lot of fresh produce to choose from. The dried mangos soak up the moisture from the onion and chiles, along with the layered spice flavors. Serve this deliciously complex chutney with roasted meat, on a turkey sandwich, or mixed into a simple rice dish.

FERMENTATION VESSEL

1 pint jar

INGREDIENTS

5 pieces dried mango, thinly sliced

2 Fresno chiles, chopped

2 medium red onions, chopped

2 tablespoons yellow mustard seed

1½ tablespoons curry powder

1 tablespoon grated fresh ginger

½ teaspoon ground turmeric

2 teaspoons pickling or sea salt

1. Combine the mango, chiles, onions, mustard seed, curry powder, ginger, turmeric, and salt in a large bowl, tossing and massaging gently until liquid pools in the bottom of the bowl.

2. Using a muddler or pounder, press the mixture down into a pint jar, pushing out air bubbles as you go. Use a fermentation weight of your choice to make sure everything stays pressed down.

3. Tightly place the lid on the jar, then place the jar on a plate out of direct sunlight and away from drafts to ferment for 10 to 14 days, tasting on day 10 to see how the flavor is developing. If you see pressure building up, burp the lid daily to release the gases. Alternatively, use an air lock on top of the jar.

4. Once it's sour enough to suit you, tightly cap the jar, transfer it to the refrigerator, and store for up to 1 year.

Get Funky: To make this chutney even spicier, replace the Fresno chiles with 8 to 10 bird's eye chiles. Don't forget to wear gloves while chopping—these babies are *hot*.

SWEET RED PEPPER RELISH

YIELD: MAKES 1 PINT

Prep time: 20 minutes, plus 45 minutes rest time • Fermentation period: 5 to 7 days
Storage: Refrigerate for up to 6 months

This mild relish is great for folks who love the fruity flavor of fresh bell peppers but don't love the heat. The natural sweetness of the bell peppers will dissipate somewhat during the fermentation as the bacteria consume the sugars; you can sweeten up the final product by adding a tablespoon or two of sugar, along with some red wine vinegar, after the active fermentation has stopped.

FERMENTATION VESSEL
1 pint jar

INGREDIENTS

2 large red bell peppers, chopped

1 large shallot, minced

¼ cup lightly packed fresh basil leaves, cut into thin ribbons

Juice of ½ lemon

2 teaspoons pickling or sea salt

Pinch freshly ground black pepper

Pinch ground clove (optional)

2 tablespoons red wine vinegar (optional)

2 tablespoons sugar, or less as desired (optional)

1. In a large bowl, combine the bell peppers, shallot, basil, lemon juice, salt, black pepper, and clove (if using), tossing and massaging gently. Cover the bowl loosely with a clean towel and let sit for 45 minutes, then massage a bit more, until liquid pools in the bottom of the bowl.

2. Using a muddler or pounder, press the mixture down into a pint jar, pushing out air bubbles as you go. Use a fermentation weight of your choice to make sure everything stays pressed down.

3. Tightly place the lid on the jar, then place the jar on a plate out of direct sunlight and away from drafts to ferment for 5 to 7 days, tasting on day 5 to see how the flavor is developing. If you see pressure building up, burp the lid daily to release the gases. Alternatively, use an air lock on top of the jar.

4. When it's sour enough to suit you, stir in the vinegar (if using) and sugar (if using). Tightly cap the jar, transfer it to the refrigerator, and store for up to 6 months.

Make It a Meal: Spread a thick layer of this relish inside a grilled cheese sandwich or mix it with light goat cheese for a probiotic cheese dip.

SOUR CORN RELISH

YIELD: MAKES 1 QUART

Prep time: 20 minutes • **Fermentation period: 4 hours to 5 days** • **Storage: Refrigerate for up to 2 weeks**

Versions of this sweet-and-sour relish are popular across the South. I remember eating sour corn as a college student in North Carolina, but I never put together that it was fermented. This ferment doesn't keep for very long, so it's best enjoyed within a couple of weeks. While it can ferment for up to 5 days, it will also be delicious after just a few hours of fermenting. Eat some fresh if you simply can't wait.

FERMENTATION VESSEL

1 quart jar

INGREDIENTS

3 cups fresh sweet corn kernels

½ cup chopped red onion

1 Fresno or other medium-heat chile, minced

½ tablespoon pickling or sea salt, plus 1½ tablespoons

1 quart unchlorinated water

1 teaspoon coriander seed, lightly crushed

1 teaspoon cumin seed

1. Combine the corn, onion, and chile in a large bowl. Add ½ tablespoon of salt and toss to combine.

2. In a quart jar, combine the water, coriander, cumin, and remaining 1½ tablespoons of salt. Cap and shake the brine to dissolve the salt completely. Make sure none of the salt remains at the bottom and no salt particles are visible in the water.

3. Pack the corn mixture firmly into a second quart jar. Make sure there is enough headspace for the relish to be completely submerged in the brine.

4. Pour the brine over the corn to cover completely. Use a piece of corncob (or fermentation weight of your choice) to keep everything under the brine. You don't want anything popping up above the brine as it will attract mold pretty quickly.

5. Place the lid on the jar, then place the jar on a plate out of direct sunlight and away from drafts to ferment for up to 5 days, tasting after 4 hours to see how the flavor is developing. A harmless white scum may form on the top. Just skim it off every day or two to keep things in balance.

continued >

— continued —

6. Once it's sour enough to suit you, tightly cap the jar, transfer it to the refrigerator, and store for up to 2 weeks.

That's Cool: Corn has its origins in Mexico, where it was first cultivated over 9,000 years ago. Indigenous farmers who preserved and cultivated heirloom varieties for their different attributes are to thank for the fact that, today, Mexico grows 59 types of corn—more than any other country in the world.

HOT EGGPLANT BASIL RELISH

YIELD: MAKES 1 PINT

Prep time: 30 minutes, plus 2 hours rest time • Fermentation period: 5 to 10 days
Storage: Refrigerate for up to 6 months

I love the way the flavors come together in this drama queen of a relish. Just when you think you've got a handle on the salty, tangy, and herbal notes, the heat from the habanero shows up to bring another layer to the party. I can truly eat this relish out of the jar by the spoonful (and frequently do). To civilize matters, use it as a stuffing for roasted bell peppers or heap it onto a crostini as you would bruschetta.

FERMENTATION VESSEL
1 pint jar (wide-mouth preferred)

INGREDIENTS

1 medium eggplant, unpeeled and cut into ½-inch cubes

1 tablespoon pickling or sea salt, plus ½ tablespoon

1 cup packed fresh basil leaves

5 garlic cloves, peeled

2 habanero chiles, seeded

1. Put the eggplant in a medium bowl and add 1 tablespoon of salt, tossing to coat evenly. Cover the bowl loosely with a clean towel and set aside to rest for 2 hours.

2. Combine the basil, garlic, chiles, and remaining ½ teaspoon of salt in a food processor. Pulse until a moist paste forms. Alternatively, use a knife to dice it all up by hand.

3. Drain the eggplant in a colander, pressing it with a spoon to release as much moisture as possible.

4. In a large bowl, combine the eggplant and chile paste, tossing and massaging gently until liquid pools in the bottom of the bowl.

5. Using a muddler or pounder, press the mixture down into a pint jar, pushing out air bubbles as you go. Use a fermentation weight of your choice to make sure everything stays pressed down.

6. Tightly place the lid on the jar, then place the jar on a plate out of direct sunlight and away from drafts to ferment for 5 to 10 days, tasting on day 5 to see how the flavor is developing. If you see pressure building up, burp the lid daily to release the gases. Alternatively, use an air lock on top of the jar.

continued >

— continued —

7. Once it's sour enough to suit you, tightly cap the jar, transfer it to the refrigerator, and store for up to 6 months.

Get Funky: If you're not a fan of the chiles' heat, replace the habaneros with half of a small red or green bell pepper. You can also use two of the multicolored mini sweet peppers sold by the bag at most supermarkets.

FERMENTED PICO DE GALLO

YIELD: MAKES 1 QUART

Prep time: 45 minutes • Fermentation period: 2 to 3 days • Storage: Refrigerate for up to 1 month

The phrase *pico de gallo* translates to "rooster's beak" and is believed to get its name from the fact that it was originally enjoyed as a finger food, picked up by two fingers pinched together to resemble the shape of a bird's beak. The verb *picar* in Spanish means "to prick or poke," but it is also used to refer to something spicy—as in, it "pokes" your tongue. Don't say I didn't warn you.

FERMENTATION VESSEL
1 quart jar

INGREDIENTS

2 pounds ripe but firm tomatoes, cored and chopped

½ pound jalapeño, serrano, or other medium-heat chiles, chopped

5 garlic cloves, chopped

1 medium red onion, chopped

1 bunch fresh cilantro, chopped

Juice and grated zest of 1 lemon

Juice and grated zest of 1 lime

1 tablespoon pickling or sea salt

½ teaspoon freshly ground black pepper

½ teaspoon ground cumin

1. In a medium bowl, combine the tomatoes, chiles, garlic, onion, cilantro, lemon juice and zest, lime juice and zest, salt, black pepper, and cumin, mixing well.

2. Using a muddler or pounder, press the mixture down into a quart jar, pushing out air bubbles as you go. Use a fermentation weight of your choice to make sure everything stays pressed down.

3. Tightly place the lid on the jar, then place the jar on a plate out of direct sunlight and away from drafts to ferment for 2 to 3 days, tasting on day 2 to see how the flavor is developing. If you see pressure building up, burp the lid daily to release the gases. Alternatively, use an air lock on top of the jar.

4. Once it's sour enough to suit you, tightly cap the jar, transfer it to the refrigerator, and store for up to 1 month.

Troubleshooting: This ferment will sometimes develop a boozy flavor from the sugars in the tomatoes that want to go right on into alcoholic fermentation. This is not harmful, but it will alter the flavor of the ferment, so it's best consumed within a month or so. If you prefer, use underripe or green tomatoes to make it last longer.

SALSA VERDE (TOMATILLO SALSA)

YIELD: MAKES ABOUT 1 QUART

Prep time: 20 minutes • **Fermentation period: 3 to 5 days** • **Storage: Refrigerate for up to 6 months**

Here is another lacto-fermented version of a Mexican classic: salsa verde. Fresh tomatillos have a bright, acidic flavor similar to a green tomato, but with an almost citrusy note. I like to use this salsa on scrambled eggs or cheese enchiladas, but it is also great with fresh corn tortilla chips for a quick snack.

FERMENTATION VESSEL
1 quart jar

INGREDIENTS

2 pounds tomatillos, papery husks removed and halved

2 garlic cloves, halved

1 medium white onion, coarsely chopped

1 jalapeño, chopped (seeded for less heat)

1 tablespoon pickling or sea salt

½ bunch fresh cilantro, coarsely chopped

1. Combine the tomatillos, garlic, onion, jalapeño, and salt in a food processor. Process on low until it reaches a chunky salsa texture, then add the cilantro and pulse to combine.

2. Transfer the salsa to a quart jar, leaving about 1 inch of headspace at the top.

3. Tightly place the lid on the jar, then place the jar on a plate out of direct sunlight and away from drafts to ferment for 3 to 5 days, tasting on day 3 to see how the flavor is developing. If you see pressure building up, burp the lid daily to release the gases. Alternatively, use an air lock on top of the jar.

4. Once it's sour enough to suit you, tightly cap the jar, transfer it to the refrigerator, and store for up to 6 months.

That's Cool: Tomatillos were cultivated by the Aztecs in Mexico as early as 900 BCE, likely even before tomatoes were grown. The word *tomatillo* translates to "little tomato" in Spanish and is based on the Nahuatl word *tomatl*.

GREEN TOMATO, CORN, AND JALAPEÑO SALSA

YIELD: MAKES ABOUT 1½ PINTS

Prep time: 20 minutes • Fermentation period: 3 to 7 days • Storage: Refrigerate for up to 1 year

This recipe is inspired by a version in Holly Davis's book *Ferment: A Guide to the Ancient Art of Culturing Foods*. I made some minor tweaks and removed the olive oil, as it can alter the pH of the ferment and potentially create conditions where the botulism toxin can grow. If you like, drizzle the salsa with a bit of olive oil before serving.

FERMENTATION VESSEL

1 quart jar

INGREDIENTS

4 large firm green tomatoes, cored and cut into bite-size chunks

1 small jalapeño, thinly sliced

1 cup fresh sweet corn kernels

2 tablespoons chopped fresh cilantro stems

2 teaspoons pickling or sea salt

1. In a large bowl, combine the tomatoes, jalapeño, corn, cilantro, and salt, tossing and massaging gently until liquid pools in the bottom of the bowl.

2. Using a muddler or pounder, press the mixture down into a quart jar, pushing out air bubbles as you go. Use a fermentation weight of your choice to make sure everything stays pressed down below the brine.

3. Tightly place the lid on the jar, then place the jar on a plate out of direct sunlight and away from drafts to ferment for 3 to 7 days, tasting on day 3 to see how the flavor is developing. If you see pressure building up, burp the lid daily to release the gases. Alternatively, use an air lock on top of the jar.

4. Once it's sour enough to suit you, tightly cap the jar, transfer it to the refrigerator, and store for up to 1 year.

CHAPTER EIGHT

SAUCES AND PASTES

You can go about making fermented sauces in two different ways: Brine your peppers whole or in large pieces, similar to the recipes in chapter 5, or grind them up into a mash before fermenting. Either way, a food processor or blender is essential for most of the recipes in this chapter. If you're on a tight budget, an immersion (stick) blender is a great option that won't take up counter space and is simple to clean. Gloves are another must for these spicy sauces—don't learn that the hard way!

ELLYN'S PROBIOTIC KETCHUP

YIELD: MAKES ABOUT 1 PINT

Prep time: 15 minutes • **Fermentation period: 2 to 3 days** • **Storage: Refrigerate for up to 6 months**

Like many five-year-olds, my niece, Ellyn, *loves* her ketchup. While she hasn't tried this version yet, I'm shamelessly naming this ketchup after her as a ploy to get some good microbes in her belly along with those French fries. This easy fermented ketchup has none of the corn syrup that commercial varieties do, making it much healthier for slathering on whatever you like.

FERMENTATION VESSEL
1 pint jar

INGREDIENTS

5 tablespoons unchlorinated water

3 tablespoons sugar

2 (6-ounce) cans low-sodium tomato paste

1 teaspoon pickling or sea salt

½ teaspoon ground mustard

Pinch ground allspice

Pinch ground cloves

3 tablespoons brine from a previous ferment

¼ cup raw apple cider vinegar

1. Combine the water and sugar in a small saucepan over medium heat. Warm, stirring frequently, until sugar is just dissolved. Remove from the heat and set aside.

2. Put the tomato paste in a medium bowl. Add the salt, ground mustard, allspice, and cloves. Stir in the sugar water, brine, and raw apple cider vinegar, mixing well. Use a spatula to scrape the mixture into a pint jar.

3. Tightly place the lid on the jar, then place the jar on a plate out of direct sunlight and away from drafts to ferment for 2 to 3 days, tasting on day 2 to see how the flavor is developing. Burp the lid daily to release the gases. Alternatively, use an air lock on top of the jar.

4. Once it's sour enough to suit you, tightly cap the jar, transfer it to the refrigerator, and store for up to 6 months.

Make It a Meal: Thin this ketchup with a bit of water to make a simple glaze for meatballs or classic meatloaf.

GARLIC HONEY

YIELD: MAKES ABOUT ½ PINT

Prep time: 15 minutes • **Fermentation period: 10 to 30 days** • **Storage: Refrigerate for up to 6 months**

Is it a sauce, a vinaigrette, or a cold remedy? By their powers combined, garlic and honey do it all in this super easy concoction with endless uses. As it ferments, the honey becomes thinner (and more garlicky, of course), while the garlic is mellowed and darkened a bit. Drizzle this on a white pizza, blend it with vinegar and oil for a honey vinaigrette, or just keep it handy as a naturally antimicrobial and throat-soothing cough remedy.

FERMENTATION VESSEL
1 pint jar (or smaller)

INGREDIENTS

1 garlic head, cloves separated, peeled, and lightly crushed

1 small dried chile (optional)

¾ cup of raw honey, plus more as needed

1. Put the garlic in a pint jar, filling it about three-fourths full. Add the chile (if using).

2. Pour the honey over the garlic, covering it completely. Stir to make sure the garlic gets evenly coated.

3. Tightly place the lid on the jar, then place the jar on a plate out of direct sunlight and away from drafts to ferment for 3 days.

4. Remove the lid and give everything a stir. Look for tiny bubbles in the honey and some slight pressure building up in the jar, which indicates that fermentation is under way.

5. Reseal the jar and let it ferment for an additional 7 to 27 days, stirring every other day and tasting after 1 week to see how the flavor is developing. The longer it ferments, the more the garlic flavor will develop.

6. Once the flavor suits you, tightly cap the jar, transfer it to the refrigerator, and store for up to 6 months.

That's Cool: When garlic is crushed, the amino acids released interact with natural enzymes to produce allicin, a compound that is lauded for its antioxidant and anti-inflammatory properties. Combining that with antimicrobial honey makes this a healing concoction for whatever ails you.

FERMENTED HOT MUSTARD

YIELD: MAKES ABOUT 1 PINT

Prep time: 10 minutes • Fermentation period: 3 to 4 days • Storage: Refrigerate for up to 6 months

Mustard is one of the easiest condiments to make at home, and yet, somehow, people always ooh and aah when you show up with homemade mustard. This fermented version is particularly well suited to clearing your sinuses, thanks to the cold process that keeps the volatile compounds in mustard at their most pungent. It will last indefinitely, but will mellow out over time, so you may want to make smaller quantities more frequently if you like it extra sharp.

FERMENTATION VESSEL
1 pint jar

INGREDIENTS

3 garlic cloves, peeled

⅔ cup unchlorinated water

¾ cup yellow mustard seed

¼ cup brown mustard seed

3 tablespoons brine from a previous ferment

2 teaspoons pickling or sea salt

½ teaspoon garlic powder

Juice of 2 lemons

1. Add the garlic, water, yellow and brown mustard seed, brine, salt, garlic powder, and lemon juice in a food processor and blend on high until the mixture takes on the texture of grainy mustard. Continue blending to achieve a smoother, creamier texture if desired.

2. Use a spatula to scrape the mixture into a pint jar, pressing down to release any air bubbles. Leave a maximum of 1 inch of headspace to minimize oxidation.

3. Tightly place the lid on the jar, then place the jar on a plate out of direct sunlight and away from drafts to ferment for 3 to 4 days, tasting on day 3 to see how the flavor is developing.

4. Transfer to the refrigerator and store for up to 6 months.

That's Cool: Mustard seeds have been used for their antimicrobial properties since the earliest days of their cultivation in the Indus River Valley. Historians believe that the Romans were the first to use them as a culinary item by mixing the seeds with freshly crushed grape juice and skins (a.k.a. *must*), which ultimately led to the name we know it by today.

NICE 'N' EASY GREEN SAUCE

YIELD: MAKES ABOUT 1 PINT

Prep time: 20 minutes • Fermentation period: 10 to 14 days • Storage: Refrigerate for up to 6 months

Here's one for the folks who like chiles for their flavor but not so much the heat. The basil and lemongrass give it a refreshing herbal lift without masking the pure chile taste. As with the Peri-Peri Fire Sauce (see page 116), I like the mash method for this recipe to better integrate the lemongrass and basil flavors.

FERMENTATION VESSEL
1 pint jar

INGREDIENTS

15 basil leaves, cut into thin strips

2 green bell peppers, seeded and cut into wide strips

2 garlic cloves, coarsely chopped

1 jalapeño, seeded and halved

1 lemongrass stalk, tender leaves only, coarsely chopped

½ tablespoon pickling or sea salt

1 cup unchlorinated water

1. Put the basil, bell peppers, garlic, jalapeño, lemongrass, salt, and water in a food processor or blender, then process until it reaches a thick saucy texture.

2. Use a spatula to scrape the mixture into a pint jar, pressing down to release any air bubbles. Leave a maximum of 1 inch of headspace to minimize oxidation.

3. Tightly place the lid on the jar, then place the jar on a plate out of direct sunlight and away from drafts to ferment for 10 to 14 days, tasting on day 10 to see how the flavor is developing.

4. Once the flavor suits you, strain the sauce through a mesh strainer to make it smoother. Alternatively, keep it chunky and tightly cap the jar, transfer it to the refrigerator, and store for up to 6 months.

EASY SRIRACHA-STYLE HOT SAUCE

YIELD: MAKES ABOUT ½ PINT

Prep time: 15 minutes • Fermentation period: 2 to 5 days • Storage: Refrigerate for up to 1 year

Make your own version of the rooster bottle classic with this super easy recipe. I like using Fresno chiles (sometimes mislabeled as red jalapeños) in this sauce for their bright red color and medium spice level. Feel free to mix it up and use whatever chiles you like, but keep in mind that the color will be murkier if you use green chiles mixed with red. For a milder version, use red bell peppers or mini sweet red peppers mixed in with the Fresno chiles.

FERMENTATION VESSEL
1 pint jar

INGREDIENTS

6 to 8 Fresno chiles, sliced lengthwise (seed for less heat)

3 garlic cloves, crushed

1 cup unchlorinated water

½ tablespoon sea salt

1 teaspoon sugar (optional)

1. Put the chiles and garlic in a pint jar. Press them down with a wooden spoon to pack tightly.

2. In a clean jar, combine the water and salt. Cap and shake the brine to dissolve the salt completely. Make sure none of the salt remains at the bottom and no salt particles are visible in the water.

3. Pour the brine over the chiles. Use a fermentation weight of your choice to make sure everything stays below the brine.

4. Loosely place the lid on the jar, then place the jar on a plate out of direct sunlight and away from drafts to ferment for 2 to 5 days, until the brine looks cloudy and smells sour. This should happen around day 2, but if your environment is a bit cooler, it may take the full 5 days.

5. Drain the brine and reserve half of it, then put the remaining mixture in a blender and blend on high until smooth. Add some of the brine back in to thin the sauce as needed. Add the sugar (if using) and blend to combine.

6. Use a funnel to transfer to a sauce bottle (or just keep it in the same jar). Tightly cap the bottle, transfer it to the refrigerator, and store for up to 1 year.

APRICOT-HABANERO HOT SAUCE

YIELD: MAKES ABOUT 1 PINT

Prep time: 15 minutes • Fermentation period: 2 to 5 days • Storage: Refrigerate for up to 6 months

Every year, I make about a dozen jars of my favorite apricot-habanero jelly to give as holiday gifts. It's become a holiday tradition in my house, and it tastes amazing with Christmas ham. This is a hot sauce version of that jelly. The apricots lend a light stone-fruit sweetness, and floral notes from the habanero temper some of the heat.

FERMENTATION VESSEL
1 pint jar

INGREDIENTS

3 habanero chiles, stemmed and cut into wide strips (seed for less heat)

1 large yellow or orange bell pepper, cut into wide strips

½ medium red onion, thinly sliced

1 cup unchlorinated water, plus more as needed

½ tablespoon pickling or sea salt

½ cup dried apricots, sliced

2 to 5 tablespoons honey or sugar (optional)

1. Put the chiles, bell pepper, and onion in a pint jar. Press them down with a wooden spoon to pack tightly.

2. In a clean jar, combine the water and salt. Cap and shake the brine to dissolve the salt completely. Make sure none of the salt remains at the bottom and no salt particles are visible in the water.

3. Pour the brine over the veggies. If needed, add a bit more water so that everything is submerged. Use a fermentation weight of your choice to keep everything under the brine.

4. Loosely place the lid on the jar, then place the jar on a plate out of direct sunlight and away from drafts to ferment for 2 to 5 days, until the brine looks cloudy and smells sour. This should happen around day 2, but if your environment is a bit cooler, it may take the full 5 days.

5. Drain the brine, reserving half of it. Add the dried apricots, then put the mixture in a blender and blend on high until smooth. Add some of the liquid back in to thin the sauce as needed. Add the honey (if using) and blend to combine.

6. Use a funnel to transfer to a sauce bottle (or just keep it in the same jar). Tightly cap the bottle, transfer it to the refrigerator, and store for up to 6 months.

Get Funky: Switch it up with a large shallot instead of the red onion. Or add a few dried hibiscus petals to punch up the floral notes a bit.

PERI-PERI FIRE SAUCE

YIELD: MAKES ABOUT 1 QUART

Prep time: 20 minutes • Fermentation period: 7 to 10 days • Storage: Refrigerate for up to 2 months

Peri-peri, piri-piri, or pili-pili—however you spell it, this fiery sauce gets its name from the blazingly hot peri-peri chile. Authentic peri-peris are difficult to find in the United States, but Thai bird's eye chiles or any small hot chiles are a good substitute. I prefer to make this one as a mash; I find that the fresh herbal flavors incorporate more uniformly that way. Wear your gloves for this one (and maybe some goggles, too).

FERMENTATION VESSEL
1 quart jar

INGREDIENTS

2 ounces (about 50) peri-peri or bird's eye chiles, stemmed and coarsely chopped

2 large bell peppers, seeded and coarsely chopped

½ cup chopped fresh cilantro

½ cup chopped fresh basil

4 garlic cloves, coarsely chopped

1 teaspoon smoked paprika

Juice and grated zest of 2 lemons

2 teaspoons pickling or sea salt

¼ cup extra-virgin olive oil

1. Put the chiles, bell peppers, cilantro, basil, garlic, paprika, lemon juice and zest, and salt in a food processor or blender, then process until it reaches a uniform chunky texture.

2. Use a spatula to scrape the mixture into a quart jar, pressing down to release any air bubbles. Leave about 1 inch of headspace.

3. Tightly place the lid on the jar, then place the jar on a plate out of direct sunlight and away from drafts to ferment for 7 to 10 days, tasting on day 7 to see how the flavor is developing. This ferment shouldn't build up too much pressure, but just to be safe, open the jar over the sink, facing away from you.

4. Once the flavor suits you, return the mixture to the food processor, blend on low, and slowly drizzle in the olive oil to emulsify it with the rest of the sauce.

5. Return the sauce to the jar, tightly cap it, and store in the refrigerator for up to 2 months.

That's Cool: Capsaicin (the compound in chiles that makes them hot) does a great job of both protecting and propagating hot chiles. The heat keeps mammals away, but birds lack the taste buds to register it. This is how seeds are spread in the wild and maybe even relates to how the bird's eye got its name—their bright colors help catch those little birdie eyes.

TURMERIC SPICE PASTE

YIELD: MAKES ABOUT ½ PINT

Prep time: 15 minutes • **Fermentation period: 7 to 10 days** • **Storage: Refrigerate for up to 6 months**

This paste makes a powerful flavor base to add to soups, stir-fries, and the like. Turmeric is beloved for its anti-inflammatory properties, but fresh turmeric can be hard to come by. All the more reason to ferment them when you do come across them. Adding a healthy dose of black pepper helps your body absorb all the good stuff that turmeric brings by increasing the bioavailability of its nutrients.

FERMENTATION VESSEL
1 half-pint jar or pint jar

INGREDIENTS

20 pieces fresh turmeric, peeled (see tip)

1 teaspoon cumin seed

1 teaspoon smoked paprika

1 teaspoon freshly ground black pepper

1 teaspoon pickling or sea salt

1. Add the turmeric, cumin, paprika, black pepper, and salt to a food processor or blender, then process until it reaches a smooth paste consistency. It will remain fairly dry.

2. Use a spatula to scrape the mixture into a half-pint or pint jar, pressing down to release any air bubbles. Leave a maximum of 1 inch of headspace to minimize oxidation.

3. Tightly place the lid on the jar, then place the jar on a plate out of direct sunlight and away from drafts to ferment for 7 to 10 days. Since this paste is meant to serve as a base, tasting for doneness is tricky. Look for a slightly darker hue and a slightly acidic smell. This ferment shouldn't build up too much pressure, but just to be safe, keep an eye on the lid for signs of pressure buildup, and burp the jar every other day to release pressure, as needed.

4. Place a piece of parchment paper or plastic wrap on top of the paste and press down to minimize oxidation. Tightly cap the jar, transfer it to the refrigerator, and store for up to 6 months.

Troubleshooting: Fresh turmeric is challenging to peel without losing half of the good stuff in the process. Use the edge of a dull metal spoon instead of a veggie peeler to peel away the soft outer skin.

LEMONGRASS LIME CHILE PASTE

YIELD: MAKES ABOUT ½ PINT

Prep time: 15 minutes • Fermentation period: 7 to 10 days • Storage: Refrigerate for up to 6 months

This aromatic paste came about as a means to feed a personal addiction of mine—to the seasoning on Trader Joe's Thai Lime & Chili Cashews. I pick up a bag of those pricey little spiced nuts every time I go and may *possibly* have been caught shaking the leftover spices directly into my mouth, Doritos-style, after the nuts are all gone. This paste is a decidedly more refined way to experience that flavor combination, with a probiotic bonus.

FERMENTATION VESSEL

1 half-pint jar

INGREDIENTS

10 bird's eye or other hot chiles, stemmed

5 garlic cloves, coarsely chopped

2 stalks lemongrass, tender leaves only, coarsely chopped

Juice and grated zest of 2 limes

2 tablespoons brine from a previous ferment

1 teaspoon fish sauce

1 teaspoon sugar

1. Put the chiles, garlic, lemongrass, lime juice and zest, brine, fish sauce, and sugar in a food processor or blender, then process until it reaches a smooth paste consistency. It will remain fairly dry.

2. Use a spatula to scrape the mixture into a half-pint jar, pressing down to release any air bubbles. Leave a maximum of 1 inch of headspace to minimize oxidation.

3. Tightly place the lid on the jar, then place the jar on a plate out of direct sunlight and away from drafts to ferment for 7 to 10 days. Since this paste is meant to serve as a base, tasting for doneness is tricky. Look for a slightly darker hue and a slightly acidic smell. This ferment shouldn't build up too much pressure, but just to be safe, keep an eye on the lid for signs of pressure buildup, and burp the jar every other day to release pressure, as needed.

4. Place a piece of parchment paper or plastic wrap on top of the paste and press down to minimize oxidation. Tightly cap the jar, transfer it to the refrigerator, and store for up to 6 months.

GREEN CHILE PASTE

YIELD: MAKES 1 QUART

Prep time: 20 minutes • Fermentation period: 7 to 10 days • Storage: Refrigerate for up to 6 months

This might be the most versatile recipe in the book: a mild to medium blend of green chiles and spices that can pivot from nachos, to curry, to a spicy chicken soup, depending on your needs. Add about ⅓ cup of this paste to a good melting cheese (or hey, even Velveeta) for a quick and easy chili con queso dip.

FERMENTATION VESSEL
1 quart jar

INGREDIENTS

4 hatch, poblano, or other mild-to medium-heat green chiles, stemmed and coarsely chopped

4 jalapeño peppers, stemmed and coarsely chopped (seed for less heat)

4 garlic cloves, coarsely chopped

1 chipotle in canned adobo sauce, coarsely chopped

1 medium white onion, coarsely chopped

1 large shallot, coarsely chopped

1 tablespoon smoked paprika

1 tablespoon cumin seed

1 tablespoon pickling or sea salt

1. Put the peppers, garlic, chipotle, onion, shallot, paprika, cumin, and salt in a food processor or blender, then process until it reaches a chunky texture.

2. Use a spatula to scrape the mixture into a quart jar, pressing down to release any air bubbles. Leave a maximum of 1 inch of headspace to minimize oxidation.

3. Tightly place the lid on the jar, then place the jar on a plate out of direct sunlight and away from drafts to ferment for 7 to 10 days. Since this paste is meant to serve as a base, tasting for doneness is tricky. Look for a slightly darker hue and a slightly acidic smell. This ferment shouldn't build up too much pressure, but just to be safe, keep an eye on the lid for signs of pressure buildup, and burp the jar every other day to release pressure, as needed.

4. Place a piece of parchment paper or plastic wrap on top of the paste and press down to minimize oxidation. Tightly cap the jar, transfer it to the refrigerator, and store for up to 6 months.

FERMENTED HORSERADISH PASTE

YIELD: MAKES ABOUT ½ PINT

Prep time: 10 minutes • Fermentation period: 7 to 10 days • Storage: Refrigerate for up to 3 months

Get out your gloves and your goggles for this one! If your horseradish is fresh, you'll know it by the way it stings your eyes and nasal passages. Although it starts out with a bang, horseradish loses its punch pretty quickly unless you acidify it, which prevents the enzymes from breaking down its heat-inducing compounds. That's where the brine from a previous ferment (or fermented hot sauce) comes in. Be sure to purée this in a well-ventilated place to avoid unnecessary tears.

FERMENTATION VESSEL
1 half-pint jar

INGREDIENTS

½ pound fresh horseradish, peeled and cut into small chunks

1 parsnip, peeled and cut into small chunks (optional)

2 tablespoons brine from a previous ferment or any fermented hot sauce

1½ teaspoons sea salt

1 teaspoon sugar

1. Put the horseradish, parsnip (if using), brine, salt, and sugar in a food processor or blender, then process until it reaches a smooth paste consistency. It will remain fairly dry.

2. Use a spatula to scrape the mixture into a quart jar, pressing down to release any air bubbles. Leave a maximum of 1 inch of headspace to minimize oxidation. Optionally, use a fermentation weight of your choice to make sure everything stays pressed down.

3. Tightly place the lid on the jar, then place the jar on a plate out of direct sunlight and away from drafts to ferment for 7 to 10 days. Since this paste is meant to serve as a base, tasting for doneness is tricky. Look for a slightly darker hue and a slightly acidic smell. If you see air pockets form, open the jar and press them out with a clean utensil.

4. Place a piece of parchment paper or plastic wrap on top of the paste and press down to minimize oxidation. Tightly cap the jar, transfer it to the refrigerator, and store for up to 3 months.

That's Cool: Horseradish has become a traditional part of Jewish Seder feasts, representing the maror, or bitter herbs, eaten to remind the faithful of their time spent in bondage.

CHAPTER NINE

COOKING WITH FERMENTATION

Combining your ferments with fresh and cooked ingredients is a great way to mellow out flavors that may be a bit too strong to enjoy on their own, especially if you're new to eating fermented foods. While it's true that cooking does kill most of the probiotic and nutrient content, new research shows that even dead bacteria (a.k.a. *post*biotics) can benefit our health. The bottom line is this: Whatever approach gets you to incorporate more fermented vegetables into your diet on a regular basis is a good one.

< Kimchi Mary (page 125)

BEET KVASS HUMMUS

YIELD: SERVES 6

Prep time: 10 minutes • Cook time: 50 minutes

This gorgeous snack combines earthy roasted beets with chickpeas and garlic. Roasting the chickpeas along with the beets softens them up for a creamier hummus texture. Adding some beet kvass after roasting retains its probiotic benefits, deepens the color, and provides a tangy note from the lactic acid. To make this even quicker, skip the roasting and use 1 can of cooked (not pickled) beets instead of the raw beets.

INGREDIENTS

2 cans chickpeas, drained

3 medium beets, peeled and cut into 1-inch pieces

4 garlic cloves, crushed

Salt

1 tablespoon extra-virgin olive oil, plus 2 tablespoons

3 tablespoons tahini (optional)

Juice of 1 lemon

¼ cup Beet Kvass (page 73)

Freshly ground black pepper

1. Preheat the oven to 350°F. Line a baking sheet with aluminum foil.

2. Put the chickpeas, beets, and garlic on the prepared baking sheet. Season with salt, then drizzle with 1 tablespoon of olive oil. Cover loosely with another layer of foil.

3. Roast for 45 minutes, or until the beets are tender and beginning to caramelize. Remove them from the oven and allow to cool for a few minutes.

4. Scrape the roasted veggies into a blender or food processor, add tahini (if using), and purée on high until the mixture reaches a smooth consistency.

5. With the processor running, slowly drizzle in the lemon juice, beet kvass, and remaining 2 tablespoons of olive oil until the mixture emulsifies into a creamy hummus texture.

6. Taste and season with salt and black pepper as needed. Store leftover hummus in the refrigerator for up to 1 week.

Make It a Meal: Grab some take-out falafel, the Israeli Salad (see page 94), a few olives, and this vibrant hummus for a quick mezze platter.

KIMCHI MARY

YIELD: SERVES 1

Prep time: 2 minutes

Here it is: the easiest recipe in the book. Featuring my own McVicker's Proud Mary Bloody Mary Mix (sold on my website) with kimchi juice and the booze of your choice, it's a fun way to get a shot of probiotics. Drink it fast, before the microbes get away!

INGREDIENTS

2 ounces gin or vodka

1 ounce kimchi juice

4 ounces McVicker's Proud Mary Bloody Mary Mix

Fermented pickle, for garnish

1. In a glass jar, combine the gin, kimchi juice, and Bloody Mary mix, along with a healthy scoop of ice. Cap and shake vigorously to mix and chill the ingredients.

2. Serve in a tall glass, garnished with your favorite fermented pickle.

Get Funky: The classic cucumber pickle is always nice, but why not switch it up with some pickled okra, cauliflower, or carrots? You can also skewer an assortment of pickled veggies for extra credit.

SLOW COOKER KAPUSTA WITH KIELBASA

YIELD: SERVES 8

Prep time: 20 minutes • Cook time: 7 hours

Kapusta is the Polish word for "cabbage," but it can also refer generally to any cabbage-based dish. This slow cooker version, flavored with kielbasa and mushrooms, makes it easy to throw together in the morning for a hearty dinner. Using Classic Sauerkraut (see page 25) will give you the most authentic version, although this is delicious with Dill Pickle Kraut (see page 36) and Apple Cider Sauerkraut (see page 38), too.

INGREDIENTS

2 tablespoons unsalted butter, at room temperature

3 bacon slices

2 large sweet onions, finely chopped

2 large portobello mushrooms, thinly sliced

1 quart Classic Sauerkraut (page 25)

½ teaspoon freshly ground black pepper

½ teaspoon dried thyme

½ cup light brown sugar

2 cups water

2 pounds kielbasa, cut into 2-inch slices

Rye or whole-wheat bread, for serving

Unsalted butter, at room temperature, for serving

1. Melt the butter in a large skillet over medium heat. Add the bacon and cook until most of the fat is released into the pan, 5 to 6 minutes. Remove the bacon from the heat and set aside.

2. Add the onions to the skillet, stirring occasionally, until the onions just begin to brown, 4 to 5 minutes. Add the mushrooms and sauté another 2 to 3 minutes.

3. While the onions and mushrooms cook, drain the sauerkraut in a colander, pressing down with a wooden spoon to release more liquid.

4. Put the drained sauerkraut, cooked onions and mushrooms, black pepper, thyme, brown sugar, water, and kielbasa in a slow cooker. Chop the bacon and add it to the slow cooker. Stir to combine, then cover and cook on high for 1 hour.

5. Reduce the heat to low and cook for an additional 6 hours.

6. Serve with rye bread and butter.

Troubleshooting: If you don't have a slow cooker, you can cook this in a Dutch oven on low, which would likely reduce the cooking time by about half.

KIMCHI STEW

YIELD: SERVES 4

Prep time: 10 minutes • Cook time: 30 minutes

This recipe comes from Samantha Paone, founder of Golden State Pickle Works in Petaluma. As a professional pickler, I tip my hat, my apron, *and* my dish towel to those intrepid fermenters like Samantha who are bringing authentic, high-quality ferments to the commercial market. Here is her recipe for kimchi stew that's perfect with a classic kimchi, especially if you have some on hand that's gone a bit too sour.

INGREDIENTS

1 large shallot, chopped

3 garlic cloves, chopped

2 tablespoons chopped fresh ginger

⅛ teaspoon pickling salt, plus more as needed

½ pound ground pork

2 cups sliced shiitake mushrooms

2 cups Traditional Baechu-Kimchi (page 46)

1 package medium or soft tofu, cut into large cubes

2 cups bone broth or chicken stock

¼ cup frozen peas

2 cups water

4 large eggs

4 scallions, white and pale green parts only, chopped

4 cups cooked rice

1. Place a 6-quart pot over medium heat. Add the shallot, garlic, ginger, and salt and sauté until cooked through, about 5 minutes.

2. Add the pork and cook, breaking up as the veggies get incorporated, for about 5 minutes, until just cooked through.

3. Add the mushrooms and season lightly with salt. Add the kimchi, tofu, broth, peas, and water and simmer for about 10 minutes.

4. Crack the eggs on top the stew and cover until the eggs are cooked to your liking, about 5 minutes if you like them on the runny side.

5. Add the scallions and stir. Serve with rice on the side, adding rice to the stew as you eat it.

QUICK KHAO SOI

YIELD: SERVES 3 TO 4

Prep time: 10 minutes • Cook time: 25 minutes

Khao soi is a noodle soup that is endlessly adaptable. In fact, the Northern Thai version that uses red curry is distinctly different from the Laotian version that features fermented soybeans and often fermented mustard greens, like the ones on page 82. Here is a general recipe that you can use with any of the pastes in chapter 8.

INGREDIENTS

4 ounces dried rice noodles

1 tablespoon coconut or extra-virgin olive oil

1 large shallot, finely chopped

2 garlic cloves, minced

2 tablespoons fermented paste of your choice

1 (14-ounce) can coconut milk

1 cup chicken or vegetable broth

1 red bell pepper, thinly sliced

2 tablespoons fish sauce

1 tablespoon soy sauce

2 tablespoons light brown sugar

1 tablespoon Easy Sriracha-Style Hot Sauce (page 114)

8 ounces tofu of choice

Juice of 1 lime

Salt (optional)

1. Bring a pot of lightly salted water to boil over medium-high heat, add the noodles, and cook according to package instructions. Drain and set aside in a colander or bowl.

2. In the same pot, heat the oil over medium heat. Add the shallot and sauté until fragrant and golden, about 3 minutes. Add the garlic and fermented paste, then cook for 1 to 2 minutes.

3. Add the coconut milk and broth and bring to a low simmer. Add the bell pepper, fish sauce, soy sauce, sugar, and hot sauce.

4. Add the tofu and simmer until heated through, about 2 to 3 minutes. Add the lime juice. Season with salt (if using).

5. Divide the noodles evenly among 3 to 4 bowls, then ladle the soup over them.

Get Funky: Try topping this with ½ cup of the Spicy Mustard Greens (see page 82).

SICHUAN PORK NOODLE SOUP WITH SPICY MUSTARD GREENS

YIELD: SERVES 4

Prep time: 10 minutes • Cook time: 30 minutes

Pork with pickled vegetables is a classic pairing in Sichuan cooking. If you've got your Spicy Mustard Greens (see page 82) ready to go, you're well on your way to making this slurp-worthy soup that comes together quickly with some pork and a few pantry items. You can leave the chiles out if the mild heat from the mustard greens is enough for you. Dried noodles will work, but if you can get your hands on fresh rice or wheat noodles, their chewy texture is extra nice with the minced pork and greens.

FOR THE PORK

1 teaspoon salt

2 teaspoons cornstarch

1 teaspoon sesame oil

1 teaspoon Shaoxing wine or regular cooking wine

¼ teaspoon freshly ground black pepper

½ pound minced pork

1 tablespoon extra-virgin olive oil

3 small bird's eye or other hot chiles, seeded and finely chopped (optional)

2 to 3 cups Spicy Mustard Greens (page 82), drained and chopped

FOR THE NOODLE SOUP

10 ounces rice noodles

6 cups chicken stock

1 tablespoon sesame oil, for garnish

1 scallion, white and pale green parts only, finely chopped, for garnish

TO MAKE THE PORK

1. Whisk together the salt, cornstarch, sesame oil, wine, and black pepper in a medium bowl. Add the pork, then set aside to marinate while preparing the rest of the soup.

2. In a nonstick pan or wok, heat the oil over medium heat until it shimmers. Add the pork and cook just until brown, about 3 to 4 minutes. Add the chiles (if using) and mustard greens. Stir-fry everything together for a 2 to 3 minutes before removing from the heat.

TO MAKE THE NOODLE SOUP

1. Bring a large pot of lightly salted water to boil over medium-high heat, add the noodles, and cook according to package directions. Drain and set aside in a colander or bowl.

2. Add the chicken stock to the pot you cooked the noodles in and bring to a low boil, then remove from the heat.

3. Divide the noodles between serving bowls and ladle in hot broth to cover. Top with the pork and mustard greens mixture.

4. Garnish with a drizzle of sesame oil and the chopped scallion before serving.

RASSOLNIK (RUSSIAN DILL PICKLE SOUP)

YIELD: SERVES 8

Prep time: 15 minutes • Cook time: 55 minutes

Although shredding pickles into your soup might sound like something born out of dorm room desperation, the resulting flavor is not nearly as strange as it may sound. In this classic Russian comfort food, pickles are shredded in small bits and cooked along with meat, barley, and vegetables. Some folks swear by this soup as a hangover cure, thanks to its heartiness and the electrolytes from pickles. You could omit the meat entirely to make this a vegetarian soup—it's got plenty of flavor to spare.

INGREDIENTS

1 tablespoon unsalted butter, cold

½ pound stew meat, such as pork shoulder or beef chuck, cut into bite-size cubes

1 medium white onion, minced

1 carrot, shredded

1 celery stalk, minced

Salt

Freshly ground black pepper

8 cups chicken or vegetable broth

2 to 3 potatoes, peeled and cut into small pieces

¼ cup pearl barley

4 Classic Dill Pickles (page 29), shredded on a box grater, divided

Splash brine from Classic Dill Pickles

Fresh dill, for garnish

Dollop sour cream, for garnish

1. In a large saucepan or Dutch oven, melt the butter over medium heat. Add the meat and cook, stirring occasionally, until browned, about 5 to 7 minutes. Transfer to a plate and set aside.

2. Add the onion, carrot, and celery to the saucepan with the meat drippings, season with salt and black pepper, and cook until the onion is translucent, about 5 to 7 minutes. If it begins to stick, add a splash of the broth to help move things around.

3. Add the broth, potatoes, and barley, then bring to a boil. Add 3 of the shredded pickles and the brine to the soup.

4. Reduce the heat to low, cover, and simmer for 30 to 40 minutes, until the potatoes and barley are cooked through. Season with additional salt and black pepper as needed.

5. Remove from the heat and garnish with the remaining shredded pickle, the dill, and sour cream.

That's Cool: Rassolnik is often traditionally made with veal or lamb kidneys. I kept them out of this version, figuring that adding pickles to your soup is probably enough adventure for one recipe.

EASY ESCABECHE QUESADILLAS

YIELD: MAKES 8 QUESADILLAS

Prep time: 5 minutes • Cook time: 20 minutes

I love to make these quick quesadillas as an easy way to combine spicy fermented escabeche veggies with the creamy flavors of melted cheese and avocado. To be honest, the humble quesadilla is a great vehicle for introducing just about any of the relishes or chopped veggie ferments in this book (kimchi quesadillas, anyone?). Use this recipe as a base for combining melted cheesy goodness with your favorite ferment.

INGREDIENTS

1 large avocado, halved and pitted

Juice of ½ lime

1 teaspoon garlic salt

8 medium tortillas

Extra-virgin olive oil, for coating tortillas (about 2 tablespoons)

2 cups shredded melting cheese of choice, divided

1 cup Escabeche veggies (page 61), divided

Fermented hot sauce or relish, for serving

1. In a small bowl, combine the avocado, lime juice, and garlic salt, then mash roughly with a fork, leaving it a bit chunky.

2. Heat a heavy skillet or nonstick pan over medium heat.

3. Brush one side of each tortilla with olive oil to coat lightly. One at a time, place the tortilla, oil-side down, in the skillet. Spread with about ¼ cup of the cheese. Spoon about 2 tablespoons of the escabeche veggies in the center, smoothing out evenly.

4. As soon as the cheese begins to melt, fold the tortilla in half down the middle. Cook, flipping every minute or so, until the cheese is all melted and the tortilla is beginning to crisp. Transfer to a baking sheet in a low oven to keep warm. Repeat the process with the remaining ingredients.

5. Serve with the mashed avocado, along with your favorite fermented hot sauce or relish.

Get Funky: Add 2 tablespoons of the Sour Corn Relish (see page 101) to each quesadilla along with the escabeche veggies for an extra sweet-and-sour crunch. Or get even spicier with a layer of Haitian Pikliz (see page 96) and Peri-Peri Fire Sauce (see page 116) for dipping.

KANSAS BIEROCKS

YIELD: MAKES 10 TO 15 BIEROCKS

Prep time: 10 minutes, plus 15 minutes to rise • Cooking time: 20 minutes

Growing up in Kansas, bierocks—meat and cabbage-filled pastries—were a popular comfort food at community gatherings, county fairs, and even my grade school cafeteria. I adapted this version from a recipe I found on a yellowed piece of newsprint in my Grandma Margarett's recipe box, clipped from the *Dodge City Daily Globe*.

INGREDIENTS

1 pound ground beef

1 cup chopped white onion

2 to 3 cups Classic Sauerkraut (page 25)

1 tablespoon all-purpose flour

2 teaspoons salt

½ teaspoon freshly ground pepper

Pinch allspice

1 (2-pound) package frozen bread dough, defrosted (or enough to make 10 to 15 rolls)

1 large egg white, beaten, for glaze (optional)

Mustard or relish, for serving

1. Grease a baking sheet and set aside.

2. In a large skillet over medium heat, cook the beef and onion for 5 minutes, or until the beef is no longer pink. Add the sauerkraut, flour, salt, black pepper, and allspice. Reduce the heat to low and simmer for another 5 minutes, stirring frequently. (If mixture seems dry, add a little water.) Remove from the heat and let the beef mixture cool slightly while preparing the dough.

3. Roll out the dough evenly, then cut into 5-inch squares (10 to 15, depending on the package of dough).

4. Place about ¼ cup of beef mixture in the center of each square. Fold in the corners and pinch together, sealing well. Put the rolls, seam-side down, on the prepared baking sheet. Let rise for about 15 minutes.

5. While the bierocks rise, preheat the oven to 350°F.

6. Bake for 15 to 20 minutes, or until the bread is nicely browned, brushing a thin layer of egg white (if using) over each bierock during the last 5 minutes of cooking.

7. Serve with mustard or your favorite relish on the side. Store in the refrigerator wrapped in aluminum foil for up to 5 days or in the freezer for up to 6 months.

PICKLE DOGS

YIELD: MAKES 4 DOGS

Prep time: 5 minutes • Cook time: 10 minutes

The genius of the pickle dog is so simple it barely warrants a recipe. But hey, I'm throwing it in here for the sheer novelty factor of turning a pickle into a hot dog bun. Using pickles that are on the larger side will give you a better shot of keeping it all contained in the "bun," though once you add some sauerkraut and fermented mustard, the (glorious) mess is inevitable.

INGREDIENTS

1 tablespoon vegetable oil

4 hot dogs, pierced with a fork

4 large Classic Dill Pickles (page 29)

Fermented Hot Mustard (page 112), for serving

Sauerkraut or other cabbage-based ferment, for serving

1. Heat the oil in a skillet over medium heat, swirling to coat evenly. Add the hot dogs and cook until slightly charred on all sides, about 5 to 7 minutes.

2. While the hot dogs cook, slice the pickles open lengthwise, leaving a bit attached like a hot dog bun.

3. Spread the inside of each pickle with the fermented mustard. Place a hot dog in each pickle, then top with sauerkraut. Serve immediately with plenty of napkins.

Get Funky: Dress your dog with any of the other following ferments: Ellyn's Probiotic Ketchup (see page 110), Classic Sauerkraut (see page 25), or Fermented Horseradish Paste (see page 120).

REUBEN FRITTERS

YIELD: MAKES 24 TO 36 FRITTERS

Prep time: 20 minutes • Cook time: 30 minutes

This recipe comes from my childhood best friend Heidi Brown, a fellow fermenter who's become masterful at finding new ways to incorporate sauerkraut into her family's meals. From Heidi: "This recipe combines two of my favorite things in the world: Reuben sandwiches and the Kansas State Fair." As such, this spin on the Reuben sandwich is balled and fried, dipped in Thousand Island dressing, and best enjoyed with friends while reminiscing about rides on Ye Old Mill and fun times in the Bier Garden.

INGREDIENTS

Vegetable or canola oil, for frying

1 pound corned beef, chopped

1 cup shredded Swiss cheese

2½ cups Classic Sauerkraut (page 25), drained

8 ounces cream cheese, at room temperature

1 tablespoon stone ground mustard

½ teaspoon garlic powder

1 cup all-purpose flour

3 large eggs, lightly beaten

2 cups panko bread crumbs

Salt

Thousand Island dressing, for dipping

1. Fill a large pot halfway with oil. Heat over medium-low to medium heat until it registers between 350°F and 375°F on a deep-fry thermometer.

2. While the oil heats, put the corned beef, Swiss cheese, sauerkraut, cream cheese, mustard, and garlic powder in a large bowl. Use a hand mixer to beat until combined. Form the mixture into balls about the size of a golf ball.

3. Set up three bowls: one for the flour, one for the eggs, and one for the panko. Dredge each ball into the flour first, then eggs, then panko. Set aside. Repeat until all the fritters are breaded.

4. Working in batches of 6 to 8, carefully drop the fritters into the pot and fry for about 5 minutes, or until golden brown.

5. Remove from the oil with a slotted spoon or small mesh strainer and set aside on a wire rack (or a baking sheet lined with paper towels) to cool. Lightly season with salt.

6. Serve warm with the dressing for dipping.

Measurement Conversions

VOLUME EQUIVALENTS (LIQUID)

US STANDARD	US STANDARD (OUNCES)	METRIC (APPROXIMATE)
2 tablespoons	1 fl. oz.	30 mL
¼ cup	2 fl. oz.	60 mL
½ cup	4 fl. oz.	120 mL
1 cup	8 fl. oz.	240 mL
1½ cups	12 fl. oz.	355 mL
2 cups or 1 pint	16 fl. oz.	475 mL
4 cups or 1 quart	32 fl. oz.	1 L
1 gallon	128 fl. oz.	4 L

VOLUME EQUIVALENTS (DRY)

US STANDARD	METRIC (APPROXIMATE)
⅛ teaspoon	0.5 mL
¼ teaspoon	1 mL
½ teaspoon	2 mL
¾ teaspoon	4 mL
1 teaspoon	5 mL
1 tablespoon	15 mL
¼ cup	59 mL
⅓ cup	79 mL
½ cup	118 mL
⅔ cup	156 mL
¾ cup	177 mL
1 cup	235 mL
2 cups or 1 pint	475 mL
3 cups	700 mL
4 cups or 1 quart	1 L

OVEN TEMPERATURES

FAHRENHEIT	CELSIUS (APPROXIMATE)
250°F	120°C
300°F	150°C
325°F	165°C
350°F	180°C
375°F	190°C
400°F	200°C
425°F	220°C
450°F	230°C

WEIGHT EQUIVALENTS

US STANDARD	METRIC (APPROXIMATE)
½ ounce	15 g
1 ounce	30 g
2 ounces	60 g
4 ounces	115 g
8 ounces	225 g
12 ounces	340 g
16 ounces or 1 pound	455 g

Resources

Fermentation Education Websites

Ferment Works (www.ferment.works)

Fermented Food Lab (www.fermentedfoodlab.com)

Phickle (www.phickle.com)

Wild Fermentation, Sandor Katz (www.wildfermentation.com)

Wellness Mama (tutorial for making whey)

(https://wellnessmama.com/2402/how-to-make-whey/)

Books on Fermentation

Fermenting Vegetables, Kirsten and Christopher Shockey

Fiery Ferments, Kirsten and Christopher Shockey

The Art of Fermentation, Sandor Ellix Katz

The Noma Guide to Fermentation, René Redzepi and David Zilber

Wild Fermentation, Sandor Ellix Katz

High-Quality Spices and Ferments

Burlap and Barrel (www.burlapandbarrel.com)

Diaspora Co. (www.diasporaco.com)

Golden State Pickle Works (www.goldenstatepickleworks.com)

McVicker Pickles (www.mcvickerpickles.com)

Oaktown Spice Shop (www.oaktownspiceshop.com)

Penzeys (www.penzeys.com)

Volcano Kimchi (www.volcanokimchi.com)

Fermentation Tools and Equipment

Cultures for Health (www.culturesforhealth.com)

FARMCurious (www.farmcurious.com)

Kraut Source (www.krautsource.com)

References

Davis, Holly. "Green Tomato, Corn, and Jalepeño Salsa." In *Ferment: A Guide to the Ancient Art of Culturing Foods*, 70. New York, NY: Chronicle Books, 2019.

Gunders, Dana, and Jonathan Bloom. "Wasted: How America Is Losing Up to 40% of Its Food From Farm to Fork to Landfill." National Resources Defense Council, 2017. Retrieved from www.nrdc.org.

Jazayeri, Katrina. "Iranian Spiced Pickles (Torshi)." *The Immigrant Cookbook: Recipes That Make America Great*, 196. Northampton, MA: Interlink Pub Group, 2017.

Jephson, Erin. "Watermelon Radish & Bok Choy Kimchi." *Putting Up with Erin*, May 6, 2014. https://www.puttingupwitherin.com/2014/05/06/watermelon-radish-bok-choi-kimchi/.

Lee, Edward. "Green Tomato Kimchi." In *Smoke and Pickles: Recipes and Stories from a New Southern Kitchen*, 167. New York, NY: Artisan, 2013.

Shockey, Kirsten K., and Christopher Shockey. "Spicy Onion-Mango Ferment." In *Fiery Ferments: 70 Stimulating Recipes for Hot Sauces, Spicy Chutneys, Kimchis with Kick, and Other Blazing Fermented Condiments*, 137. North Adams, MA: Storey Publishing, LLC, 2017.

Syhabout, James, and John Birdsall. "Fermented Chinese Mustard Greens in Rice Brine." In *Hawker Fare: Stories & Recipes from a Refugee Chef's Isan Thai & Lao Roots*, 302. New York, NY: Anthony Bourdain/Ecco, 2018.

Index

Acknowledgments

Big love and thanks to everyone at The Ruby, especially the Fermenters Club, for providing a heartfelt community willing to brave the mysteries of the microbes with me. Thanks to my work family at WorkshopSF: Kelly Malone, David (DK) Knight, and Hayley Corbeill for creating a magical DIY space where the fermentation-curious can come together and learn. Thanks to Sam Eichner for his skillful editing, and to everyone at Callisto Media for guiding me through my first book with ease.

I'm deeply grateful to Sandor Katz for introducing me, and so many others, to the magic of fermentation via his books. Anyone can write a recipe, but it takes a special person to unearth the meaning behind it all, and to communicate it so beautifully. Thank you to Kirsten and Christopher Shockey for sharing their finely tuned palates and passion for fermentation via their excellent books, from which I've learned so much.

Alejandro Morales, thank you for cooking me breakfast, bravely tasting my experiments, and generally keeping me (mostly) sane throughout the writing process, and always. Thank you to the San Francisco Public Library for providing me and my fellow San Franciscans with a beautiful, safe, and (mostly) quiet place to learn. Heidi Brown, thank you for the fritters, and for 30 years of friendship. Iso Rabins, thank you for the encouragement and for keeping me on track, teammate!

I'm forever grateful to Roxy Esquivel for teaching me how to make Costa Rican tamales and fielding my many questions about Tico cuisine with patience and love. Most important, thanks to my parents, Earl and Molly McVicker, for their constant love and support, and especially for gently reminding me that I've always loved writing.

About the Author

Kelly McVicker is an educator, pickle maker, and entrepreneur. As founder of McVicker Pickles, she has developed custom pickles for clients, including Shake Shack and Creator Burger. Her award-winning pickled creations have been featured on restaurant and bar menus across San Francisco. Kelly's popular workshops on fermentation, home canning, and other food preservation techniques help people discover the joys of preserving their own food safely and deliciously. A certified Master Food Preserver, she has presented at food festivals and fairs across the United States, including a speech at TEDx entitled "Pickling and the Art of Time Travel." Kelly lives in San Francisco, along with an abundance of pickled things that she expects will come in handy during the next earthquake.

CPSIA information can be obtained
at www.ICGtesting.com
Printed in the USA
LVHW071507200220
647644LV00016B/1425

9 781646 115266